DEMOGRAPHY

This is a volume in the Arno Press collection

DEMOGRAPHY

Advisory Editor
Kingsley Davis

Editorial Board
Harley L. Browning
William Petersen

See last pages of this volume
for a complete list of titles

ILLEGITIMACY

AND THE

INFLUENCE OF SEASONS UPON CONDUCT

TWO STUDIES IN DEMOGRAPHY

BY

ALBERT LEFFINGWELL

ARNO PRESS

A New York Times Company

1976

Editorial Supervision: SHEILA MEHLMAN

———••◦∞◦••———

Reprint Edition 1976 by Arno Press Inc.

Reprinted from a copy in
  The University of Illinois Library

DEMOGRAPHY
ISBN for complete set: 0-405-07980-X
See last pages of this volume for titles.

Manufactured in the United States of America

Publisher's Note: The frontispiece, as well as
the maps between pp. 28-29 and 62-63, have been
reproduced here in black and white.

———••◦∞◦••———

Library of Congress Cataloging in Publication Data

Leffingwell, Albert, 1845-1916.
   Illegitimacy and the influence of seasons upon
conduct.

   (Demography)
   Reprint of the 1892 ed. published by Swan
Sonnenschein, London, Scribner, New York, in Social
science series.
   1. Illegitimacy--Great Britain. 2. Crime
and criminals--Great Britain. I. Title. II. Series.
HQ999.G7L5 1976   301.32'1   75-38134
ISBN 0-405-07987-7

ILLEGITIMACY

AND THE

INFLUENCE OF SEASONS UPON CONDUCT

ILLEGITIMACY

AND THE

INFLUENCE OF SEASONS UPON CONDUCT

TWO STUDIES IN DEMOGRAPHY

BY

ALBERT LEFFINGWELL, M.D.

Member of the International Congress of Hygiene and Demography

WITH MAPS AND DIAGRAMS

London

SWAN SONNENSCHEIN & CO.

NEW YORK: CHARLES SCRIBNER'S SONS

1892

BUTLER & TANNER,
THE SELWOOD PRINTING WORKS,
FROME, AND LONDON.

PREFACE.

THE present volume contains the first treatise in the English language, upon the subject of Illegitimacy. On the Continent this phase of social phenomena has attracted considerable attention ; but investigations have been chiefly confined to countries possessing comparatively little interest for the English reader.

The following pages are devoted largely to a consideration of illegitimate births in the different sections of the British Isles.

The second essay is an attempt to present to the reader certain phenomena of periodicity in human conduct and mental disease, which, although for many years familiar to students, are still comparatively unknown to the general public. To what extent the hypothesis advanced accounts for all the facts observed, each student must judge for himself. At all events it is believed that the statistics herein for the first time grouped together will be of permanent interest.

The writer has aimed to present some statistics of human conduct, now buried in official reports, in such a way as not only to be easily intelligible but also interesting. He believes it a mistake to imagine that facts must necessarily be dull, or figures dry. No romance evolved from the imagination of the novelist can ever compare with the tragedies of real life. What we wish to know is where to find the truth, and how to interpret it.

To what extent, then, the reader may ask, can confidence be placed in the accuracy of the statistical

facts herewith presented ?   How may they be verified?
What are the sources from which they have been derived ? Do they represent original investigation or
have they been copied from other works ?

Each tabular statement in this volume relating to
Great Britain is the result of personal research and
reference to the original official sources of information,
—excepting only in one or two cases where the contrary is stated.   The annual rates of Illegitimacy, for
instance, in different sections of the country are derived
from the reports of the Registrar-General.   The
authority for all other statistical averages is usually
given in the text.   An opportunity for personal verification of diagrams and tables is largely afforded by
the detailed statements contained in the Appendix.

To insure the highest degree of accuracy, every
tabular statement presents the statistics of several
successive years.   It is conceivable for instance, that
one might mistake in calculating the illegitimacy of
Scotland as about three times that of Ireland,—taking
a single year as a basis.   It is infinitely improbable
that precisely the same error should be repeated in a
dozen calculations, over a dozen years.   While the
author believes that even slight inaccuracies will
not be found in the transcription of the figures herein
contained, he is certain that no error sufficient to
invalidate conclusions can possibly have occurred.

To Mr. F. Finch, of the General Register Office,
Somerset House, the author is indebted for valuable
assistance.

A. L.

4, *Regent Street,*
    Oxford.

CONTENTS.

STATISTICAL TABLES.

ILLEGITIMACY:

A STUDY IN MORALS.

––––––

AGAINST the background of history, too prominent to escape the observation from which it shrinks, stands a figure, mute, mournful, indescribably sad. It is a girl, holding in her arms the blessing and burden of motherhood, but in whose face one finds no traces of maternal joy and pride. There is scarcely a great writer of fiction who has not somewhere introduced this figure in the shifting panorama of romance, appealing for pity to a world which never fails to compassionate imaginary woes; now it is Effie Deans in the Heart of Midlothian; now Fantine, resting by the roadside with Cosette in her arms; or Hester Prynne, pressing little Pearl against the scarlet letter, as she listens from the pillory to the sermon of Mr. Dimmesdale. Who is this woman so pitiable, yet so scorned? It is the mother of the illegitimate child. By forbidden paths she has attained the grace of maternity; but its glory is for her transfigured into a badge of unutterable shame.

It might be thought that a social phenomenon so universal, yet so sad, would not be left chiefly to the pen of the novelist or poet; and that more frequently some endeavour would be made to fathom cause and seek prevention of an evil so nearly affecting human happiness. Perhaps because regarded as the unmentionable in social life, illegitimacy has been so lightly passed over by serious literature. But a phase of human experience touched by the genius of Scott, of Goethe, of Victor Hugo, and Nathaniel Hawthorne, need not be shuffled out of sight as too repulsive for consideration.

In its relation to modern society, the subject of illegitimate births presents itself as a problem for scientific investigation; a problem, too, bristling with inquiries of the utmost interest. To what extent, for example, does it prevail among the most civilized people? How is it affected by poverty and destitution? Is it checked by the diffusion of education and increased by ignorance ? Is it influenced by religion, and may we detect any difference in the deterring suasion of diverging creeds ? Is the phenomenon a constant factor in a nation's birth-record year after year ? Is it increasing or decreasing ? What is the influence of race, of legislation, of public sentiment ?

These are certainly questions of interest ; but the replies thereto are, for the most part, inaccessible to the general reader. Let us see to what extent they may be answered by an investigation of facts.

Every science of to-day is based upon the accumulation of observed phemonena. No clever hypothesis, no imposing array of venerable opinions, may serve as the substitute for actual knowledge ; and when this is wanting and observation impossible, science is satisfied to confess its ignorance. Now, statistics, when gathered without other object than to record events as they occur, are of peculiar and special value. They are the record of events ; not the building of hypotheses. In contemplation of them we stand, as it were, in audience with Truth itself, as distinct from that vague shadow of truth which the best opinion and most careful estimate—apart from the facts themselves—can only be to us.

But, if the truth, are they the whole Truth? To what extent is their value vitiated by errors and omissions? Of course absolute accuracy cannot be hoped, especially in respect to an event involving so much of shame and disgrace. Concealment and infanticide undoubtedly make the record everywhere less frightful than its awful reality. But taking the statistics afforded by governmental reports, we may be almost certain that they are now gathered with such absolute indifference to results as should always characterize the search for truth; and that, apart from concealment, the errors in our day, at least, are so infinitesimal in number as not in any appreciable degree to impair their value.

Of this there is one remarkable proof, to which the attention of the reader cannot be too frequently directed; *it is the persistence of the phenomena year after year*, with but slightly varying difference. This is one proof of accuracy in statistical evidence, for it is highly improbable that precisely the same error would repeat itself over a series of years. Science is inclined to doubt the alleged phenomenon that is not and cannot be repeated ; the physician places little reliance on the drug which continually varies in effect. For, as a rule, Nature presents us with uniform continuity in the operation of her laws ; and we learn to expect from their operation, in any given period of time, not merely order, but a certain degree of persistence of repetition and invariableness. When, therefore, we discover that any event in human conduct is, year after year, so regular in appearance, so uniform in number, as almost to justify prediction for years to come, we may be almost certain that we are studying the effect of law. Take, for example, the number of illegitimate births, returned ₺y the Registrar General of Births, Deaths, and Marriages, in each of the three principal divisions of the United Kingdom. [*See Table* I.]

This is certainly a remarkable exhibit. No one can study it, or note the even steps with which, year after year, this histcry of shame and sorrow repeats itself for over a quarter of a century, without a certain feeling of awe. Here is an event, involving in forty thousand English homes a certain degree of social ruin and disgrace ; yet it recurs again and again, year after year, in almost precisely the same numbers, in almost exactly the same average frequency ! Let the eye glance, for instance, on the figures representing the number of illegitimate births in England and Wales, say in 1879, and then let us try for a moment to

TABLE No. I.—ILLEGITIMATE BIRTHS IN ENGLAND, SCOTLAND, AND IRELAND SINCE 1879.

	England.	Scotland.	Ireland.
1879	42,189	10,727	3,367
1880	42,542	10 589	3,203
1881	43,120	10,484	3,198
1882	43,155	10,546	3,268
1883	42,646	10,114	3,049
1884	42,667	10,439	3,199
1885	42,793	10,680	3,218
1886	42,838	10,506	3,079
1887	42,134	10,365	3,181
1888	40,730	9,968	3,124
1889	40,627	9,643	3,049

bring before the mind some conception of the suffering and sorrow ; of the apprehension and dread; of the sense of immeasurable disgrace, felt not only by mothers themselves, but by relations and friends, which this vast number of unlawful and unblessed births occasioned on

every side. Forty-two thousand, one hundred
births registered as illegitimate !—almost three
times as many children as are born in all the
homes of Liverpool and Birmingham every
year! Let us picture to ourselves the influence of these sad examples of frailty; the
warnings which they occasioned; the moral
each one pointed; the admonitions it enforced;
the resolutions they occasioned; and then estimate, if we can, the probable effect all this
might be supposed to have in diminishing the
evil in years to come. Then drop the eye a
line lower to the figures for the next year; and
there is the same story of trouble and disgrace;
the same number of births, increased less than
one per cent., meets our gaze. The suffering,
the unspeakable dread, the anguish, the remorse
has been doubled; the record is the same. We
take the story of another year, and then the
next, and how little is the variance! Why is
this monotone of sorrow unbroken? Why is
the tithe so pitiless in uniformity? For Nature
does not more surely guarantee to the farmer
the average product of his field than she gives
to England, to Scotland, to Ireland, this annual
harvest of sorrow and shame.

In the study of facts like these, it seems to me difficult not to see the uniform operation of natural laws in the government of human action. We look in vain for evidence of the free play of volition, untouched by motives, undetermined by cause. Surely, if any step is ever made with the misgivings that would accompany an act of will, it would be that taken by so large a number of unmarried women in commencing relations involving consequences so serious throughout life ; and we should suppose that by no possible method could science determine the results of human choice governed by motives apparently so inscrutable. Yet precisely the contrary is true. *We can predict;* and prediction of that which is to happen in future, is the test of science. With quite as much certainty as the Chancellor of the Exchequer calculates the average income of his budget a few months in advance, can the statistician predict the number of illegitimate births which will occur for years to come. Certain exceptional circumstances may conceivably arise to disturb or vary the result, precisely as a war or a famine might overturn every calculation of Mr. Gladstone or Mr. Goschen ; but the chances of such an event are very small. How many women in England and Wales, the great majority of whom are to-day in innocent and happy girlhood, will hold in their arms in 1893 the unwelcome offspring of shame ? Impossible to say ? Why, we cannot conceive that the number will be so few as 25,000, unless some awful convulsion of Nature, an earthquake, a famine, or the plague, shall destroy our population by the hundred thousand ; or some great war or invasion disturb society to its very foundation. Making every allowance for the action of agencies which is steadily and happily decreasing this social evil, we can hardly conceive of a lower number than 35,000 illegitimate births in 1893 and 1894. The actual number will probably be nearer 38,000. Or to predict with yet greater precision, we may say, that of every thousand children born in England and Wales during the year 1893, at least 42 or 43 will be illegitimate. So assuredly can we depend upon the uniformity of the laws that govern human conduct, that we know what results will occur through passion and folly for years in advance.

No imaginable human agency except war

could by the year 1892 or 1893 lower the ratio of births out of wedlock to, say, thirty per thousand. Without a sudden revolution in moral sentiment equally impossible, the rate of illegitimacy could not rise in this country to sixty per thousand in so brief a period.

I have little doubt, that during the few remaining years of this century, the rate for England and Wales will vary between forty-three and forty-eight per thousand births. Illegitimacy therefore is an example of human action, based apparently upon the fluctuating impulses of passion, involving the exercise of all that we call "free will" in one of the most important emergencies of individual life, yet, on the whole, governed by fixed and immutable laws. Hidden beyond present knowledge, unknown, and possibly as unknowable, are the ultimate causes of all phenomena, whether it be the course of a planet in its orbit, the fall of an apple to the earth, or the uniformity of human action from year to year. Perhaps, however, it is possible to discover some of the proximate circumstances which apparently regulate this special manifestation of illicit conduct.

The differences in this respect to be observed among the people of different nationality, opens a field for investigation to which I shall refer hereafter. We are in the habit of ascribing all disparity of conduct or morals existing among different populations to a variety of causes and special influences. With the great majority of us it is a fixed though unwritten creed, that nearly all the immorality of this world might be eradicated in some way by the general diffusion of knowledge, the increase in national wealth and prosperity, and, above all, by the more general acceptance of our own special and particular form of religious belief. The problem hardly admits of so easy solution. What, for instance, are we to make of differences in this respect among people of allied and intermingled lineage, guided by the same Government, living side by side in the same latitude, speaking the same language, holding to the same standards of moral obligation? The most interesting of problems is suggested by this inquiry. Any one who examines the comparative frequency of illegitimate births occurring, say, in England, Scotland, and Ireland during a term of years, can hardly fail to be impressed by the singular differences to be observed. The number of children born outside the marriage relation in each country does not permit that comparison we require; it is necessary that we ascertain what proportion these illicit births bear to the total number of children born.

The following table therefore is of special value since it indicates the prevalence of Illegitimacy in each of the three divisions of the United Kingdom for a period of years.

TABLE II.—OF EACH THOUSAND CHILDREN BORN IN ENGLAND, SCOTLAND, AND IRELAND, HOW MANY WERE ILLEGITIMATE?

Year.	Ireland.	England.	Scotland.
1878	23	47	84
1879	25	48	85
1880	25	48	85
1881	25	49	83
1882	27	49	83
1883	26	48	81
1884	27	47	81
1885	28	48	85
1886	27	47	82
1887	28	48	83
1888	29	46	81
1889	28	46	79

Here is the record for more than ten years ; and curious enough we find it. Year after year, of each thousand births in Scotland, there are almost twice as many illegitimate as in England and Wales; and more than three times as many as in Ireland. Even if this were an exceptional phenomenon it would command attention ; but it is almost the invariable rule, extending over an entire decade, and going back, it may be, for centuries, in the past. What conclusions are we to gather from these facts ? That the peasant mother of Ireland is more solicitous for the chastity of her daughters than her sisterhood of Scotland and England ? Are the precepts of virtue more highly prized and effectively inculcated in the mud-cabins of Mayo, than beneath the thatched roof of the Highland cotter ? Or is superior virtue the result of education ? Why, the Irish peasantry are steeped in ignorance, as compared with the labouring population of North Britain. Shall we infer that vice and poverty go hand-in-hand ? But an Englishman would not kennel his dogs in such cabins as I have seen in Achill and Western Ireland. Can it be the effect of religious training and influence ? But Scotland

rejoices in the open Bible and the right to
private judgment; while Ireland submits her
conscience to the control of her priesthood and
the guidance of an Infallible Church. I have
no intention to dismiss with a phrase or a sur-
mise any of these conditions or circumstances;
if their influence is here apparently questioned,
it is simply that the reader may perceive some
of the difficulties of the problem which check
all attempts at any off-hand solutions.

But another singular fact confronts us. Not
only has each great political division of Europe
its special illegitimacy average, which it repeats
pretty regularly year after year, but each de-
partment and county, each city and neighbourhood, has its own particular tribute of bastardy,
which, with almost unfailing regularity, it con-
tributes to the sum-total of the nation! Ireland,
for instance, does not differ more widely from
England or Scotland than its counties differ
from each other; and although the variance
from a uniform rate for a county is a trifle
greater than for a nation, yet the figures are
fairly steady from year to year. For instance,
let us compare certain English and Welsh
counties, showing specially high rate, with

other parts of England. In this table the
annual ratio is given for several successive
years :—

TABLE III.—To 1,000 Births in Different Sections of
England and Wales how many were Illegitimate
during a Period of Ten Years?

Divisions and Counties.	1879.	1880.	1881.	1882.	1883.	1884.	1885.	1886.	1887.	1888.	10 Years Average.
Shropshire . .	76	80	82	79	84	85	91	82	81	80	82
Cumberland. .	77	81	79	76	72	71	75	79	72	78	76
Hereford. . .	68	74	75	78	79	67	77	80	74	85	76
Norfolk . . .	77	79	75	78	73	70	70	72	73	74	74
Westmoreland .	72	71	73	84	67	71	62	69	64	69	70
North Wales .	71	67	63	68	67	68	69	75	73	73	69
All England	48	48	49	49	48	47	48	47	48	46	48
Devonshire . .	48	45	47	46	48	46	48	46	48	46	47
Somerset. . .	44	46	44	47	44	43	42	42	41	41	43
Hampshire . .	45	44	46	42	43	42	43	41	41	43	43
Kent	43	40	44	45	43	44	43	43	43	44	43
Surrey . . .	37	38	42	38	39	41	44	41	40	43	40

This is the record of ten years. Every
year one section of the country pays twice the
tribute of another part ; and yet both sections
are equally under English laws, English customs, English civilization. What, one may
well ask, are the influences, the circumstances,
the conditions, which produce such surprising
contrasts between the social morality of Devon
and Norfolk, or Surrey and Shropshire ?

But England is not the only country where

a wide divergence of morality may be observed.
In Ireland the contrast between different counties is even greater than elsewhere in the
United Kingdom. In Scotland the average
ratios of comparative prevalence of illegitimacy
are everywhere high, yet not everywhere alike.
For instance, compare the rate prevailing for
many years in the following sections of Scotland :—

TABLE IV.—OF EACH 1,000 BIRTHS IN DIFFERENT PARTS OF
SCOTLAND, HOW MANY WERE ILLEGITIMATE?

Ten Counties having for Scotland a Low Rate of Illegitimacy	Annual Rate to 1000 Births.			Ten Counties having a High Rate of Illegitimacy	Annual Rate to 1000 Births.		
	10 Years 1876–85.	1886	1887.		10 Years, 1876–85.	1886.	1887.
Ross & Cromartie	47	48	49	Nairn	106	146	94
Shetland Isles . .	52	53	45	Roxburgh . . .	108	94	108
Dumbarton . .	54	52	49	Caithness . . .	108	121	127
Renfrew . . .	59	54	58	Kincardine . .	125	123	124
Orkney Isles . .	62	65	79	Aberdeen . . .	137	142	135
Bute	66	65	67	Kirkcudbright .	146	150	154
Stirling	66	67	65	Dumfries . . .	147	138	137
Sutherland . . .	68	48	71	Elgin	153	149	149
Fife	68	64	63	Wigtown . . .	158	162	181
Lanark	69	65	68	Banff	164	162	165
Average of the 10 Counties . .	61	58	61	Average of the 10 Counties .	135	139	137

Now, these differences are altogether too
uniform to permit the hypothesis of mere

accident or chance. The same singular phenomenon may be detected by comparing the different provinces, departments, or cantons of Italy, France, Switzerland, and Germany, or the subdivisions of every large State of Europe. We are justified, I think, in assuming that these divergencies, so marked in moral action and so uniform in appearance year after year, are due to some potent causes acting continuously, yet with varying force, in the different communities of the same nationality.

I have hitherto alluded only to the more common method of measuring illegitimacy, which consists in ascertaining the proportion of children born out of legal wedlock in every thousand births. While this test is fairly accurate, and is the most ready method for judging the underlying moral sentiment locally prevailing, there is yet another comparison which is sometimes possible: I mean, the number of illegitimate children born annually to each thousand unmarried females at the child-bearing age. For instance, in 1881 the census of Scotland showed that there were then living in that portion of the kingdom

C

492,454 unmarried women (that is, spinsters and widows), between the ages of 15 and 45. During the ten years 1878–1887 there were born in Scotland 105,091 illegitimate children, or an annual average of over 21 to each thousand unmarried females at this specified age. In England and Wales the corresponding number of the unmarried females was 3,046,431 ; and the number of illegitimate births during same period was 426,184, or 14 to each thousand of the possible mothers. In Ireland the number of unmarried women at this age was a third larger than in Scotland, or 731,767. Yet to each thousand of these were born every year less than 5 illegitimate children, during a ten-year period, 1878–1887. Here again we are perplexed with the problem why Scotia and Hibernia should present such widely different contrasts. Every year in Scotland there are *five times the proportion* of bastards that see the light in Ireland ! Or, if we throw the figures into a diagram, and carry them out into decimals, we shall see the result as follows :—

TABLE V.—TO EACH THOUSAND UNMARRIED WOMEN (WIDOWS
AND SPINSTERS) BETWEEN THE AGES 15–45, HOW MANY
ILLEGITIMATE CHILDREN WERE BORN ANNUALLY, 1878–
1887?

Country.	Rate of Illegitimacy.	Proportionate Scale.
Ireland .	4·4	
England and Wales	14·0	
Scotland	21·5	

I have spoken of the persistency of these
differences year after year. Is any break of
continuity discoverable ? Let us take, for
instance, a county or group of registration
districts which, at the present time, contrasted
with some other localities, displays what, to
put it mildly, we may call a lessened sensitiveness to moral injunctions. Year after
year its rate of bastardy is considerably above
the average for all England, and far exceeds
that prevalent in other parts. Has this been
the same for the past twenty, thirty, fifty
years ? Have Norfolk, and Shropshire, and
Cumberland, not to speak of others, kept their
undesirable pre-eminence ever since any knowledge of their moral status was available ?

And how far back through the past centuries has that stream of tendency been flowing? Unfortunately, our ancestors paid but little attention to the slow gathering of dry facts. The moral condition of English life, say for the past three hundred years, we know only by the pictures of men and manners drawn by novelist and dramatist; in the adventures of Tom Jones or the perils of Pamela. It is hardly fifty years since the first attempt was made in England to get foundation facts about its moral condition in this respect.

Now, *a priori*, what should we say would be the story they reveal? Can we make the least guess as to the prevalence of illegitimacy forty or fifty years ago, or estimate the regions of greater or less proclivity? Not if all this is due to chance, independent of the law of causation. But if social phenomena depend upon the conjoint action of forces which have been continuously at work, then we should expect to discover that the area of least and the area of greatest tendency to immoral relationships are almost exactly the same, even if we contrast epochs separated by nearly half a century.

TABLE VI.—Of Total Births, How Many of each
Thousand were Illegitimate at Different
Epochs? England.

English Counties.	1842.	1862.	10 years' average 1863–1872.	10 years' average 1879–1888.	1889.	1892.
Cumberland .	114	113	110	76	79	
Hereford . .	106	80	82	76	77	
Norfolk . .	99	105	101	74	69	
Westmoreland	93	112	95	70	72	
Shropshire .	93	98	94	82	79	
ALL ENGLAND	67	63	59	48	46	
Hampshire .	64	55	51	43	42	
Kent . . .	63	55	49	43	43	
Somerset . .	62	57	54	43	37	
Surrey . . .	52	47	41	40	39	
Devon . . .	51	54	58	47	43	

It may be stated as a rule, that in English
counties where an abnormally high rate of
illegitimacy prevailed in 1842, it has prevailed
ever since ; that in counties where the average
was then less than for all England, it is less to-
day ; and that these peculiar differences have
been in existence without great variation from
one another, for almost half a century. For how
much longer, we cannot say. Unrecognised
and unsuspected, they have probably been in
existence for centuries.

And the same phenomenon is discovered if we compare the rates of illegitimacy in different sections of Scotland since 1855, when the first registration of these births was carried out. I shall refer to this hereafter in speaking of one great and most probable cause of the phenomena. It suffices to say now, that wherever in Scotland loose relationships were discovered to be frequent in 1855 and 1856, there they are found to be frequent now ; and that wherever the rates of illegitimacy were then least, they are least to-day. Even from the first these discrepancies attracted attention, as a problem for which no solution seemed to present itself. Writing as far back as 1858, in the Report of the Registrar General, Dr. Stark says : " It would be a very interesting and instructive subject to inquire what are the peculiarities in manners and morals among the inhabitants of those counties where illegitimacy is so very high as compared with the manners and morals of those counties in which illegitimacy is low. That there must be some great differences no one can doubt when the results are seen so visibly as that *one county regularly furnishes nearly twice the proportion of illegitimate births of the other.*" When these words were written this phenomenal regularity had been observed but three or four years, and it has since continued for more than thirty years.

What are the special causes of illegitimacy, especially of its widely different prevalence among communities and nations? We are justified, I have said, in assuming that such causes prevail. If all mankind were alike in temperament, disposition, preferences and habits, there could be no such manifest dissimilarity between different people as is now found in their regard for truthfulness, or their sense of honour: in their reverence for womanhood, regard for the rights of others, or the value placed upon human life. It is certainly a fair hypothesis of all that is abnormal in human conduct, which ascribes it, upon the whole, to variations in character, in organization and environment; to the stress of temptation and the vitality of deterrent forces. Of course we cannot regard illegitimate births as a standard for anything like absolute measurement of moral delinquency. In some countries of Europe, marital infidelity may be far more frequent than in others, and coexist with a low ratio of births out of marriage. This is possible; yet the excuse can hardly be maintained as applicable to differences between the inhabitants of the same country, living precisely under the same civilizing environment. We cannot thus account for the contrast between Brittany and Normandy for instance, not to mention a hundred others. And so as between nations, the value of this theory — that the concealed sin on the one hand invariably counterbalances the notorious delinquency of the other—must be somewhat doubtful. It is not true that people are all alike, except in ability to conceal their vices. Differences in conduct absolutely and truly exist. Why ? Why should one people be better or worse than another in this one respect ? That is the problem before us.

Of the causes generally supposed to be the principal factors in the production of vice and crime,—Poverty, Ignorance, and the contaminations of great cities, stand among the first. Let us very briefly examine the potency of these as predisposing to the prevalence of illegitimacy.

I. Poverty.

There can be no doubt that wealth, or at least a competence, does secure to its possessors certain safeguards against temptations, which assail not only the hungry and homeless, but those who are struggling for daily bread. The domestic servant has a poorer chance than the daughter of her mistress; the seamstress, bending over her needlework twelve hours a day, is not on an equality of temptation with those for whose pride and folly she wastes her life. It is therefore probable that in many cases the pinch of poverty does weaken the barriers against temptation. Charles Kingsley indeed has made the poacher's widow thus excuse her children's shame :—

> " We quarrelled like brutes, and who wonders ?
>   What self-respect could we keep
>   Worse housed than your hacks and your pointers,
>   Worse fed than your hogs and your sheep ?
>
> " Our daughters, with base-born babies,
>   Have wandered away in their shame ;
>   If your misses had slept, Squire, where they did,
>   *Your daughters might do the same !* "

And yet it is perfectly evident that poverty of itself does not predispose to vice or to looseness of morals. We hardly need statistics in proof of this, and yet they most potently confirm the general belief. If we look at those sections of the United Kingdom where poverty is most hopeless and pressure for the barest necessities of life the strongest, it is there, in very many instances, that we find the least tendency to illicit relations, so far as these are measurable by their most natural result. In Ireland, for example, we find the rate of bastardy is less than that in England or Scotland. Yet no one can question the misery in which the Irish peasantry has been steeped for centuries. But some parts of Ireland are exceptionally poverty stricken, and some sections, measured by an Irish standard, exceptionally prosperous. Two counties, Mayo and Down—one on the bleak and barren coast of the Atlantic, the other in prosperous Ulster, —each containing by the census of 1881 about the same number of inhabitants, present a contrast which is worth a moment's special study.

Of the relative prosperity of the two sections we may obtain a fair idea through the Irish census of 1881. Four classes of dwelling houses were enumerated. Houses of the fourth class were defined as " built of mud or

perishable materials, with only one room and
one window;" homes, we may say, unfit for
human habitation, and equalled only by the
dwellings of the most barbaric tribes. The
third class included houses of similar character
but somewhat better built, of less perishable
materials, and containing more than a single
room or a single window. Houses somewhat
superior to these constituted the remainder.
Now in 1881 in County Mayo *more than three-
fourths of the population* were enumerated as,
occupying dwellings of the third and fourth
classes. In County Down scarcely one-third
of the people were equally impoverished. In
Mayo but little over one-eighth of its surface is
susceptible even to cultivation, and forty per
cent. is either barren or bog. From personal
observation of many lands, I know of none
where nature seems to have so strongly leagued
with misrule to make prosperity impossible, as
in Mayo, Ireland. In County Down, on the
other hand, only eight per cent. of the land is
intractable to the husbandman ; and nearly half
its total area is actually under tillage.

Now, how do these two sections of the same
country differ in that sentiment of morality

which at least tends to prevent illegitimate
births? In order that the student may have
opportunity to reach his own conclusions, the
figures for ten years are given in the table
below.

TABLE VII.—COMPARISON OF ILLEGITIMACY IN TWO IRISH
COUNTIES (DOWN AND MAYO) DURING 10 YEARS,
1879–1888.

County.	No. of Illegitimate Births each year.										
	1879	1880	1881	1882	1883	1884	1885	1886	1887	1888	Total.
Mayo	31	51	29	34	33	28	36	23	30	27	**322**
Down	337	287	328	322	284	269	312	322	331	292	**3084**

I have carried out these figures for so long
a period that the reader may see that the
phenomenal preponderance of bastardy in
Down was persistent year after year. Compare now the proportion of these births to the
total number born :—

County.	Total Births 10 years, 1879–88.	Total Number of Illegitimate Births.	To 1,000 Total Births, how many illegitimate?
Mayo (Con-naught) . .	57,141	322	**5·6**
Down (Ulster)	60,346	3084	**51·1**

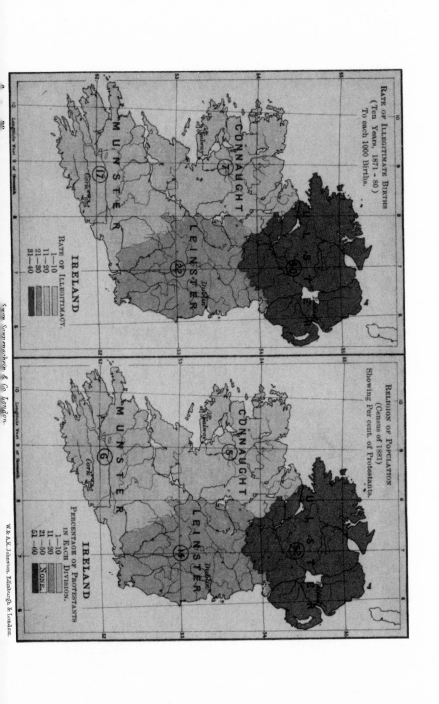

RATE OF ILLEGITIMATE BIRTHS
(Ten Years, 1871 - 80)
To each 1000 Births.

CONNAUGHT
7

MUNSTER
17

Cork

LEINSTER
22

Dublin

ULSTER
26

IRELAND
RATE OF ILLEGITIMACY.
1—10
11—20
21—30
31—40

RELIGION OF POPULATION
(Census of 1881)
Showing Per cent. of Protestants.

CONNAUGHT
5

MUNSTER
6

Cork

LEINSTER
14

Dublin

ULSTER
52

IRELAND
PERCENTAGE OF PROTESTANTS
IN EACH DIVISION.
1—10
11—20
21—50
51—60
NONE.

Longitude West 9 of Greenwich

Longitude West 8 of Greenwich

From Sonnenschein & Co. London.

W & A.K. Johnston, Edinburgh, & London.

What do these figures reveal ? On the one hand we have a section of prosperous and happy Ulster, wherein the average rate of illegitimacy for ten years was 51 per thousand births, greater than that in England and Wales ; while the wretched land of barrenness and bog shows a ratio less than any county in England, Scotland, or Ireland, and possibly less than elsewhere in Europe! If we look at the relation between illegitimate births and the unmarried and nubile womanhood between ages of 15 and 45, we shall see a somewhat modified result, yet practically the same.

	No. of Unmarried Women living between ages of 15–45.	To 10,000 Unmarried Women 15–45, how many illegitimate births annually during ten years, 1879–88 ?
Mayo (Connaught)	29,069	11
Down (Ulster) . .	34,330	90
ALL IRELAND . .	731,767	44

I shall not at this point attempt any explanation of these figures, suggestive as they are to every thinker. They certainly do not imply that destitution, hunger, and chronic wretchedness are provocative of immorality; although on the other hand it would perhaps be too great a stretch of scientific imagination to regard them as excitements to virtue.

The same fact I have observed in Scotland, in France, in Italy, in Switzerland, and it exists probably throughout Europe. Not that poor districts are invariable the most virtuous; they are not. But there is nowhere such uniform relation between the indigence of a people and the prevalence of illegitimacy, as to justify the hypothesis that this phrase of moral delinquency in any district or country can be accurately described as caused by its poverty.

II. COUNTRY AND TOWN LIFE.

The wickedness of cities, and the virtues of rural populations, have been a theme for dramatists of every age. To some extent there is justification for the common belief. Crime, as a trade, best flourishes in centres of population; the professional burglar or thief seeks companionship in guilt amid the slums of a great city; the country girl "in trouble" would perhaps hide her shame in town. It may be doubted however, whether, in proportion to total population, the percentage of the vicious is so much greater in cities than in rural communities. Is the virtue of chastity far more highly prized by the peasant? It is not made evident by statistics. The great cities of England nearly all show a proportion of illegitimate births below the rate prevalent in certain agricultural and rural districts, inhabited by an honest, sober, industrious and estimable population. Contrast, for instance, the number of illegitimate in every thousand births as they occur in the three principal cities of England, with the rate which obtains in some of the most beautiful of rural resorts.

TABLE VIII.—CITY AND COUNTRY. TO 1,000 BIRTHS, HOW MANY WERE ILLEGITIMATE?

	1885	1886	1887	1888	1889	1890	1891
LONDON . . .	40	38	40	38	38		
BIRMINGHAM .	40	43	50	53	45		
LIVERPOOL . .	61	61	66	57	58		
North Wales .	69	75	73	73	71		
Westmoreland .	62	69	64	69	72		
Cumberland .	75	79	72	78	79		
Shropshire . .	91	82	81	80	79		

It may be said that in large cities many such births escape registration and are put down as legitimate.   This of course may be possible to some extent, but I should hardly think that it could account for these differences to any degree.   For if the rate of bastardy in Shropshire or Cumberland was universal throughout England, it would mean an addition every year of thirty thousand illegitimate births to the total for England and Wales.

It is a singular fact that not only counties but far smaller sub-divisions of counties sometimes exhibit a perverse and violent tendency toward illegitimacy.   The worst districts show a rate nearly double that of England and Wales.   I was curious to ascertain how long this peculiar pre-eminence in bastardy had adhered to certain circumscribed localities ; and in the following table I give the average of five recent years (1884–1888) for the worst districts of England and Wales.   It is interesting to compare the present condition of affairs with the tendency noted by the Registrar-General, nearly half a century ago.

In regard to this table the reader will at once note several peculiarities.   In every one of these rural districts the proportion of bastardy is exceedingly high, in nearly all of them more

Table IX.—Of each 1,000 Births, how many were Illegitimate in the following Registration Districts of England and Wales during periods mentioned below?

Name of Registration District.	County.	Annual Average 1884–1888 (5 years).	1842.
Longtown . . .	Cumberland .	177	172
Alston	,,	132	125
Clun	Shropshire . .	122	109
Rhayader . . .	South Wales .	121	145
Brampton . . .	Cumberland .	117	172
Pwllheli . . .	North Wales .	114	76
Lllanfyllin . . .	,, ,,	103	80
Church Stretton .	Shropshire . .	98	109
Downham . . .	Norfolk . .	96	86
Docking . . .	,, . .	96	104
Bromyard . . .	Hereford . .	96	125
Machynlleth . .	North Wales .	93	80
Anglesey . . .	,, ,,	89	78
Newtown . . .	,, ,,	95	103
Walsingham . .	Norfolk . .	83	104
ALL ENGLAND .		47	67

than double the rate of England as a whole. Half a century ago the rate of illegitimacy *in every one of these districts was also higher*, and in most cases far higher, than the average of the country at large. There are therefore certain sections of England and Wales where every sixth or seventh or eighth child is a

L

bastard! Yet every one of these districts is at some distance from any great city. It is a curious fact that in three English counties adjoining each other, the rate of illegitimacy seems to increase in proportion to their distance from London, and this peculiarity goes back many years.

TABLE X.—TO EACH 1,000 BIRTHS, HOW MANY WERE ILLEGITIMATE ?

County.	1842	1851	1852	Ten years' Average. 1879–1888.
Essex . . .	53	69	71	34
Suffolk. . .	81	88	81	57
Norfolk . .	99	111	114	74

Is rural life then favourable to these illicit relationships? One can hardly affirm this at present. There may be a tendency to change of residence by young women in trouble from cities to their country homes, or from rural neighbourhoods to the city streets. How far these counterbalance each other one cannot say. Probably the equilibrum is not much disturbed either way, since changes of habitation are impossible to the great mass of the lower orders. In large towns there is possibly more.

of vice and dissipation than in the country; at all events it is there more concentrated and obvious. The statistics I have gathered certainly would indicate that a singularly lax theory of sexual morality obtains in some of the most secluded and remote districts of England, Scotland and Wales. One little district where for many years about one in every seven children was born illegitimate,[1] rejoices in perhaps the longest and most unfamiliar name in Great Britain—Llanfihangelytraethau. If the same rate of illegitimacy obtained throughout England as is maintained annually in this sylvan retreat, the number of such births in this country would be increased by more than 75,000 every year!

III. INFLUENCE OF EDUCATION.

What influence upon moral sentiment can we ascribe to the general diffusion of secular education? A generation ago the theory that ignorance was the great cause of vice and crime became an accepted axiom. Statistics were pressed into service; it was shown that the majority of

---

[1] The rate of illegitimacy in this district during five years (1884–1888) was almost exactly 133 per thousand; three times that of England and Wales.

criminals could not read or write; and this educational defect was assumed to be, in a great measure, the cause of their tendency towards vicious and depraved livelihood. To some slight extent the theory may possibly have been correct; but so far as illegitimacy is concerned, I doubt if we can detect any certàin deterrent influence in rudimentary education. Districts or countries where a high standard of elementary education prevails do not appear to maintain any marked pre-eminence of morals above their more ignorant neighbours. If the theory were true which ascribes a moral influence to secular learning, then in every land where the ability to read and write is most widely possessed, we should expect to find a decreased rate of bastardy as compared with nations where popular education has made no headway.

But the facts generally are most absolutely opposed to this hypothesis. If we study the map of Europe, we find that many countries where popular education is widely diffused among all classes, such as Denmark, Norway and Sweden, Prussia, Saxony, and Scotland, show a high rate of illegitimacy, while in some others, such as Russia and Ireland, the rate is very low. Even in the same country, and under the same laws, we do not find that virtue and the spelling book are invariably associated. Many years ago it was observed that in Scotland "the counties which show the highest proportion of illegitimacy are the counties which are in the highest condition as to education; while, on the other hand, the counties which produce the fewest illegitimate births are those where education is at the lowest ebb." [1] That was written nearly thirty years ago, but no change in the annual phenomenon has been since observed. Take one curious instance. Of the number of women married in Kirkcudbright, a county in southern Scotland, 99 per cent. are able to write their names in the marriage register; showing a larger proportion of women thus far educated than in any country of Europe or any county of England or Wales. Yet the rate of bastardy which there annually prevails is, year by year, greater than in any one of the 89 departments of France, Paris only excepted! This is not a solitary instance.

---

[1] See Reg. Gen. Report for Scotland, for the year 1862.

During the ten year period, 1879–1888, there
was not a single year in which the rate of
illegitimacy was not four times as high in Ulster
as in Connaught; yet in which province is
education more general? In France, putting
Paris aside, those departments where ignorance
of the alphabet is most general, are in many
cases the very ones which hold the virtue of
chastity in highest esteem. Finisterre for example, of the 89 departments of France, stands
first for the ignorance of the male population
and first for the illiteracy of its women; yet its
rate of illegitimacy during the period observed
was but 34 per 1,000 births; less than that
which prevailed during the same time *in any one
of the counties of England, Wales, or Scotland.*

We have now passed in rapid review some
of the imputed causes of this departure from
social morality, and tested by the evidence of
facts they fail to account for the different moral
standards which in different localities tend to
prevail. We cannot ascribe this laxity of conduct
to poverty, since it least manifests itself where
destitution and want have fixed their strongest
hold. The absence of secular education is not
a sufficient cause. In the great centres of

commerce and manufacture it has not such rate of prevalence as we observe "far from the madding crowd" in the secluded villages of the Lake Country, or among the hills of Wales. What then are the causes ? Surely it is no blind Fate which has thus cursed the Saxon, the Swede, and the Dane; it is no peculiar "predestination" to evil-doing that gives to Scotland its unfortunate pre-eminence. Some agencies are continually at play to create that divergence which never fails to excite the wonder of the student while contemplating the record of facts. And while I cannot claim that the evidence suffices to make doubt no longer possible, it seems to me that the wide and apparently irreconcilable differences which exist in regard to the local prevalence of illegitimacy, may be ascribed, with so strong degree of presumption in their favour as to make it "a working hypothesis," chiefly to three great causes. These are :—

    I. Religion.

   II. Legislation, and legal impediments to marriage.

 III. Heredity, or the influence of race and ancestry.

I. RELIGION.

The effect of religious belief upon human conduct is beyond question. At every age of the world's history it has influenced legislation, incited or repressed warfare, and tended on the whole to solidify and crystallise the best elements of advancing civilization. As I propose hereafter to treat the larger question of its influence as a restraint against vice and crime, it is, perhaps, needless now to anticipate the argument there to be advanced, or the conclusion to be reached. But some reference must be made to one of the most potent of agencies in checking the passions and proclivities of the human animal.

Granting its immense force upon human conscience, in the abstract, does its power depend in any sense upon the truth of its dogmatic teaching? At first glance there seems to be no question about it. Nearly every one who may read these pages is convinced that his own particular system of belief is the true basis of a sound morality: that the world would be all the better if they could adopt his creed; and that to the unsound theology of corrupt systems of faith we must ascribe the moral

failure of a wicked world. Is this overstated ?
Is there any reader who admits that another
system of belief than the one he cherishes
would make him a better man ?

It may be of interest for the student—whatever his religious faith may be—to test for
himself, by reference to the tabulated statements
he may find in these pages, the question of
relationship between a true creed and that
conduct which should be its invariable result.
Does he believe, for instance, that the highest
appreciation of chastity depends upon the
spiritual acceptance of Calvinistic theology ; in
reverence for the sanctity of the Sabbath, and
abhorrence of the Papacy ? Let him ponder
over the statistics of Scotland, and explain
why this land of strictest Sabbath-keeping and
purest Calvinism exhibits double the illegitimacy of England every year. Does he hold
that the pre-eminent excellence of the theology
of Martin Luther is evidenced by the morality
of its believers ? Let him study the records
of Norway, Sweden, and Denmark, where
Lutheranism for centuries has held undivided
sway. Does he claim that the infallible creed
of the Roman Catholic Church insures its ad-

herents superiority in morals? Then upon this hypothesis he must explain why Austria and Bavaria are so low down on this scale. Is it, then, to believers in the thirty-nine articles of the Established Church of England that we are driven to look for freedom from frailty? But where in England is the rate of illegitimacy so low as in Russia or in Greece,—not to speak of Ireland at her side?

In the face of paradoxes like these it would seem almost a contradiction of terms to assert Religion as one of the great efficient forces regulating and controlling the conduct of human passion. We know that its effect is infinitely great in individual cases; how then, we ask, does each phase of faith seem in certain instances to lose its hold? In another work the question will be discussed and a solution suggested. That in every age the religious sentiment of humanity has exerted a very powerful influence upon conduct cannot be questioned; although it may be doubted how far this influence, so far as the great seething mass of human beings are concerned, is not generally subordinate to the other and even stronger forces that move humanity toward action.

II. LEGISLATION.

A favourite maxim with a certain school
of writers is that the State cannot make
men moral by Act of Parliament. So far
as this apophthegm is intended to imply that
legislation cannot and does not influence conduct for right or wrong, it is contradicted by
universal experience. In every instance it is
the State that makes of an act a crime. As
I write, a member of the House of Commons
expelled from Parliament, is undergoing a term
of imprisonment for an act which he might
have done with impunity up to a few years ago.
Then, the English conscience being aroused,
Parliament made a new crime. Poaching,
for instance, is wrong in England, but not in
America; the law of the land makes the
offence. A blind man begging on the steps
of St. Paul's in London would be taken into
custody as a vagabond ; before the Church
of the Holy Sepulchre in Jerusalem, or of
St. Peter's in Rome, he receives his tribute of
coppers, and commits no offence. It is equally
within the power of the State to erase from its
statute book every distinction of birth ; to make
all children legitimate. It is possible, because

it has been done. Two sovereigns that once occupied the throne of England, daughters of Henry VIII., were both illegitimate as far as the law could make them, but by the first Act of her reign, Mary hastened to erase the stigma against herself. Lord Kames tells us that in 1707, Iceland having become almost depopulated by an epidemic, the King of Denmark issued a proclamation, making legitimate all children born thereafter in the island, to this extent, that no unmarried mother was to be deemed to have lost her reputation until her progeny exceeded six! The effect may be imagined.

While in Utah some years since, a lady showed me a photograph of a large group of girls about the same age. At first glance I took them to be classmates of a school. "They are some of my husband's daughters," she explained, "the three at the right are my own." Custom, religion and local laws, made them then and there legitimate children.

In what way does legislation influence the rate of illegitimacy? I think we may say in the first place—that *every impediment to marriage* tends to increase illicit relationships. It does

not at all follow that these restrictions are
unwise, or should be abolished. In Bavaria,
at one time, no young man was permitted to
marry until he could prove reasonable ability
to support a family ; and Bavaria, twenty-four
years ago, stood first in Europe for the proportionate number of its illegitimate births.
In various European countries the young man
must not marry until he has completed his
military service. In France, consent of parents
is a legal necessity up to a certain time. In all
countries legal marriage costs money, not much,
but yet something ; and a growing inclination
is everywhere noticed among the working
classes of the Continent to dispense with all
ceremonies and simply go to house-keeping.
Dr. Bertillon has estimated that in Paris there
are probably no less than 80,000 homes where
the parents are living in harmony, and educa-
ting their children, married in every sense of
the word, except that they refuse to obtain the
sanction of either Church or State. But their
children are illegitimate. In Italy, another and
very sad phase of illegitimacy is the result of
the present struggle between Church and State.
To the pious Catholic, marriage is a sacrament

which needs no sanction from human government to make it valid. But in the eye of the law
marriage is simply a civil registration, without
which no sacraments or ceremonies of religion
can make cohabitation other than illegal. Unfortunately, hundreds of poor girls have relied
solely on their religious marriage, only to find
themselves mothers of bastard children whose
legal rights the law cannot acknowledge.[1] Yet
the State is quite within its rights in demanding
civil registration as a needful adjunct to religious
ceremony. The trouble is that in Italy the
Church is at war with the State.

In England too, the law makes relationships
illegitimate, which are perfectly regular in other
parts of the English-speaking world. Children
of a deceased wife's sister are bastards in
England, yet legitimate everywhere else in
Australia, in Canada, and in the United States.
In some communities the tendency is to make
all sexual relationships legitimate, if no legal
impediment exists. No ceremony of any kind
whatever, civil or religious, is necessary to constitute a legal marriage in the State of New

[1] See the "Story of Ida," with introduction by John
Ruskin.

York. If two parties, living together, speak of each other as husband and wife, this public acknowledgment is all that is requisite to constitute their relation in the eyes of the law, a perfectly valid marriage, always supposing that there be no previous relationship of the kind. Yet children born from such a union, and legitimate in New York, are counted as bastards by every nation of Europe. The State is here supreme, and the wish of the people is the State.

I think it perfectly evident that if throughout Europe all obstacles to marriage were abolished; if parental prudence were given no power to oppose ; if all that is necessary were simply the registration of intention before a public official qualified to take acknowledgments, an act of recognition obtainable at all times, publicly or privately, by rich or poor, *without fee or cost of any kind*, it would undoubtedly add to the greater frequency of the legal tie among the poorer class, and decrease in very great proportion the prevalence of illegitimate births.

To what extent is illegitimacy increased or modified by the legal opportunity which in some countries exists of proving paternity and legitimizing the offspring? The two things are not the same. England permits the search for the putative paternity, but refuses to admit the bar sinister ever to be rubbed out. In Scotland, on the contrary, marriage of the parents makes a bastard legitimate. Does this possibility of reparation lead to greater frequency of ante-marital faults? Possibly, to some extent, though I should doubt if it had so much influence as is often supposed. This reparation by marriage can be nearly always made before the child is born; and if not made during pregnancy in spite of all pleading, the chance of its being made afterwards must be so slight that its influence I should think would be equally insignificant.

Somewhat otherwise must be the effect of refusing or permitting to a girl-mother any legal right of imputing the paternity of her offspring. In the majority of countries of Europe this inquiry may be made; in a few, it is entirely refused, and the mother must expect to bear the burden and responsibility for herself. The certainty that the father of her child need never be called upon for the least assistance would naturally, we should think, influence hesitation. Doubtless it does to some extent, but the influence is far from producing uniformity, and cannot be very strong. Compare, for instance, the prevalent rate of illegitimacy in countries permitting or refusing this right of inquiry.

Table XI.—To 1,000 Children Born, how many were Illegitimate during the period of Five Years (1878–82)? Stillbirths not Included.

Countries where inquiry as to paternity is refused.	Rate to 1,000 Births.	Countries where inquiry as to paternity is allowed.	Rate to 1,000 Births.
Belgium . . .	77	Austria . . .	143
France . . .	74	Saxony . . .	127
Italy	73	Bavaria . . .	132
Holland . . .	30	Sweden . . .	101
Russia. . . .	28	Denmark . . .	101
		Scotland . . .	84
		England & Wales	48
		Switzerland . .	47
		Ireland . . .	25

It is probable that certain forces here neutralise each other.

The highest rates of illegitimacy are certainly found where research for paternity is allowed ; but then also and in the same group, are countries whose rate is exceedingly low. The

E

refusal seems almost a gratuitous cruelty, even if it be like capital punishment in cases of theft —somewhat of a deterrent.

III. HEREDITY.

But of all causes of human conduct, one of the most potent is probably the predisposition that lies wrapped in organization, and which is passed onward by inheritance. That races as well as individuals differ in mental and moral tendencies as well as in physical characteristics, seems to have been recognised from the dawn of history. The earliest conquerors of neighbouring or distant tribes must have noted that one clan was war-like, another timid and treacherous; one people easy to bring under subjection, another impatient of restraint and quick to rebel. There appears thus to be a tendency in human nature for propensities and virtues to become crystallized, and for proclivities, active for generations, to become in some way fixed elements of character and physique. It is a trite saying that "civilization is but a thin crust over innate barbarism;" and now and then the world stands aghast when this savage love of cruelty, this hereditary viciousness breaks through all restraints, and the savage stands revealed to himself. No two nations of Europe—probably no two nations in the world—are alike in love of decency, in appreciation of virtue, in proclivities to vicious indulgence, or in subjection to moral and religious restraints. That one may see how complete is this difference, I have drawn up the following table from the facts presented by Dr. J. Bertillon, but re-arranged in order of least prevalence of illegitimate births, during the period named, to the total number of children born. (See next page.)

If these peculiar differences were unevenly fluctuating from year to year, it would be impossible to explain them on the hypothesis of heredity. But the phenomena is persistent. It has existed as far back as accurate facts have been at our disposal. Changes are going on ; in some nations the rate is possibly rising, in others it is certainly falling. The progress in either direction, measured by single years, is comparatively slow.

It will be noted that, with few exceptions, the Northern nations of Europe of Scandinavian or Teutonic origin, apparently show the strongest proclivity to those ante-marital irregularities of

TABLE XII.—COMPARISON OF ILLEGITIMATE BIRTHS AMONG PRINCIPAL NATIONS OF EUROPE (FIVE YEARS, 1878–1882).[1]

Country.	Prevailing Religion.	To 1,000 Births how many were illegitimate.	To each 10,000 women unmarried over 15, how many illegitimate births per year.
Ireland . .	*Roman Catholic*	25	31
Russia . .	*Greek ,,*	28	——
Holland . .	{ *Two-thirds Protestant* }	30	66
Switzerland .	{ *Nearly equally divided* }	47	74
England and Wales . .	*Protestant*	48	103
Italy . . .	*Roman Catholic*	73	169
France . .	*,, ,,*	74	109
Belgium . .	*,, ,,*	77	139
Prussia . .	*Lutheran*	77	182
Norway . .	*,,*	82	146
Scotland . .	*Calvinism*	84	151
German Empire .	{ *Two-thirds Protestant* }	89	206
Denmark . .	*Lutheran*	101	203
Sweden . .	*,,*	101	158
Saxony . .	*,, 96%*	127	343
Bavaria . .	*Roman Catholic*	132	295
Austria . .	*,, ,,*	143	330

[1] For the averages of this table I am indebted to the paper of Dr. Jacques Bertillon, read before the International Congress of Hygiene and Demography, at Vienna.

which illegitimacy is a sort of gauge. Why should it be so prevalent in Norway, Scotland, Iceland, Sweden, Finland, Denmark, Prussia, Saxony, Austria and Bavaria? Why does Holland stand almost alone on the Continent? We cannot ascribe it to her religion, for look at Saxony! We are dealing here not with worn-out or effete civilizations, nor with peoples given over to mad indulgence, and blind to all restraints. I venture to believe that partly in local customs, partly in existence of impediments to early marriages, partly to causes connected with religion, but most of all to the inheritance of Race and the proclivities of immediate ancestry we must look for any satisfactory explanation of these curious differences. Of course it needs constantly to be borne in mind that the rate of illegitimacy is no standard whatever of upper-class morals, and that in some countries an immense amount of marital infidelity occurs, yet leaves nothing for the statistician to record. But everywhere, too, the upper and prosperous classes are less in number than the great mass of the people, and regarding these, it is a tolerably fair exponent.

Chiefly upon hereditary predisposition or

organization, persistent through successive generations of families, I am inclined to ascribe in great measure that most remarkable phenomenon to which allusion has been made ; I mean the persistent and wide difference in moral stamina apparent in sections of the same country. It is a tenet of the national faith, that the morals of an average Englishman are better than those—let us say, of a Neapolitan or a Turk ; but what of differences between North and South England, or between East Anglia and Wessex ? They are all English, influenced by the same religion, governed by the same code of laws; why then do they differ ? Dr. Jacques Bertillon has pointed out that a line drawn on the map of France between Normandy and Brittany, and running south-easterly to Lyons and Geneva, very accurately divides those departments of France where illegitimacy is largely prevalent from those where it is comparatively rare; and singularly, this is also a line of demarcation between the races that are supposed to have intermingled in the blood of the Frenchman of to-day. Now it has been suggested by high authority that the different degrees of moral susceptibility in this respect

which we discover in England to-day may be
due to heredity; to the different strains of English blood, making themselves felt in individual
conduct even after a thousand years of unity as
a nation. Sir George Graham, writing many
years ago, first pointed out in a paragraph that
I have never seen quoted, this singular correspondence. " Excluding London," he says, "it
may be inferred that generally the unmarried
women in the counties south of the Thames,
comprising the descendants of the old Saxon
population, have few illegitimate children;
Wales stands next in the scale ; the West Midland, the N.W, and the South-Midland counties, covering the area of ancient Mercia, present
less favourable results; while in Yorkshire, the
Northern counties and the North Midland counties, covering the area of the ancient Danish
population, the number of illegitimate children
is excessively great.[1] "

This is undoubtedly a bold hypothesis. We
are accustomed to think of English blood as
homogeneous and intermingled by this time;
and to expect to trace certain influences to

---

[1] 14th Annual Report of the Registrar General, p. 13.

Danish blood a dozen centuries after the Danish invasion seems improbable enough. I am by no means disposed to account for all the divergence between North and South England by this theory.; yet the hypothesis possesses one remarkable advantage : *it explains phenomena* otherwise inexplicable.

Every student of English history is aware of the multitudinous origin of this English race : the Celt, the Roman, Angles, Jutes, Saxons, Danes, and Normans, each has stamped his impress on our features, or infused within our commingled blood some specialisation of character, some tendency towards virtue or vice. But granting this, it by no means follows that the commingling has been everywhere equal or uniform. For centuries, the great mass of the people in any locality must have been fixed to the soil by their poverty and occupation, almost as absolutely as the serfs of Russia before their emancipation. Travel was beyond their means, and the necessity for daily bread must have kept them steadily to their daily tasks. It seems very probable that the admixture of race, upon which we lay so much stress, may indeed have been far less than we

have supposed among the greater mass of
the people. The working-class population of
Norfolk or Yorkshire for example, may very
probably have exceedingly little intermixture of
the blood that pervades the Englishry of Corn-
wall or Somerset. They differ, not merely in
dialect—which tells its own story—but in ancestry, in history; and while some commingling
of all races has undoubtedly occurred among
the wealthier and more privileged classes, it has
not been sufficient very greatly to disturb the
inherent tendencies and characteristics of each
particular tribe.

But can these ancestral proclivities announce
themselves in the conduct of to-day? It is
quite conceivable, I think, without any great
violence to probability. Suppose, for instance,
that a thousand years ago, upon part of the
English coast—not then England—there de-
scends a horde of piratical adventurers. They
delight in blood and warfare; they toss the
captive infants from spear to spear; they have
no regard for chastity—indeed, they have little
reverence for any religious constraints whatever.[1] They take possession of the land, en-

[1] "Bede tells us how the Saxons fastened on Essex,

slave the conquered, and become gradually, after a few generations, fixed to the soil.[1]

Now it is quite within bounds of possibility that from the first conquest, bastardy may have been regarded among the people of such a tribe with much greater lenience than by another and more civilised tribe; that the stigma should be less, and the chance of complete reparation of character by marriage be always more probable. Every neighbourhood of such a community for generation after generation would contain a certain large proportion of the illegiti-

---

Surrey, and Wessex; how the Angles coming from Anglen (the true old England) founded the mighty kingdoms of East Anglia, Mercia, and Northumbria. Fearful must have been the woes undergone by the Celts at the hands of the ruthless English heathen, men of blood and iron. The few Celtic words admitted to the right to English citizenship . . . seem to show that the Celtic women were kept as slaves, while their husbands, the old owners of the land, were slaughtered in heaps."—Oliphant's "Old and Middle English," p. 19.

[1] Mr. Green, in his "Conquest of England," tells of these warriors who "drove mothers to slavery, and tossed babes in grim sport from pike to pike." One of our conquerors, indeed, was specially nicknamed by his companions because he absolutely refused to join in the sport of tossing children on pikes.—Green's "Conquest of England," p. 55.

mately born ; laxity of morals, as we understand the phrase, becomes evidenced by frequent events ; the custom is an inheritance of proclivity, and an example that is too common to deter.   Let this state of affairs go on for centuries, unnoticed by any comparison with other localities, now increased by wars and rebellions, now lessened a little, let us hope, by the precepts and influence of the Church ; and when, after a thousand years, science through statistics looks at last at the very heart and life of a nation's morality, it might expect to discover in localities, subject for centuries to such influences, and among people of such an origin, an especially high rate of illegitimate births.   That something like this has happened is at least probable.   One tribe of our common ancestors were pirates, and piracy was never provocative of domestic virtue.

Quite as curious, and even more vivid in some respects, is the picture which is presented by the statistics of Scotland for the last thirty-five years, and to which I have before referred. When the first detailed report of the Registrar General for the year 1855 was published, it appears at once to have attracted attention.

Certain counties of Scotland were found to present then a higher proportion of illegitimate births than in any part of France—Paris only excepted. They have maintained this singular pre-eminence ever since. Not only that, but this peculiar tendency toward loose and illicit relationships seems confined to certain counties and groups of counties—which we might almost call infected districts, so distinctly are they marked off from other sections of the country. Let us study one of them.

The counties into which Scotland is subdivided may be grouped together according to their geographical situation. One of these sections, a little cluster of five counties in the Highlands, honoured by the residence of royalty and enlightened by a University, is known to the Registrar General as the North-Eastern District. Rivalled only by the southern counties which border on England, this North-Eastern group stands above all other parts of Scotland for its ratio of illegitimate births. See, for instance, how uniformly this district has maintained its peculiar prominence for many years, when compared with another group of counties lying side by side.

TABLE XIII.—SCOTLAND : OF EACH 1,000 BIRTHS, HOW
MANY WERE ILLEGITIMATE ?

	1857	1858	1867	1868	1877	1878	Ten Years 1876–1885.
North-Eastern Counties .	145	146	145	153	139	139	141
North-Western Counties .	57	61	61	61	65	59	64

There was no country in Europe, which in 1877 and 1878 exhibited the proportion of illegimate births prevailing in North-Eastern Scotland, with the sole exception of Austria, where the rate was 140 in the last-named year.

If the reader cares to consult a map of Scotland he will see no special reason why such differences should exist. The North-Western district is composed of Ross, Cromartie, and Inverness. The North-Eastern district comprises the counties of Banff, Elgin, Nairn, Kincardine, and Aberdeen ; the five forming a promontory jutting out toward Scandinavia.

Now why do these two sections differ, and differ so enormously ? Why does one locality persistently and regularly pay twice the tribute of bastardy of its neighbour, year after year,

decade after decade—possibly century after
century ?

It is not due to ignorance, for as recently as
1878, it was found that in this North-Eastern
division only 6 per cent. of the women who
married were unable to write, while in the
' North-Western ' region the females were so
ignorant that only 38 per cent. of the whole
number who married could sign their names.
It is not due to poverty, for there was in no part
of Scotland so small a percentage of the population living in cottages of a single room.   It
cannot be due to religion, for they both cherish
the same stern faith of Calvin and Knox.   It is
not caused by any surplus of women, as some
have suggested, for between the ages of fifteen
to forty-five, there is a larger proportion of unmarried females in other parts of Scotland
where illegitimacy is far less.   Nor is it due to
any centralised predominance of vicious tendency in any one part of this promontory.   On
the contrary, the general proclivity seems to
diffuse itself over the entire region with great
evenness of distribution.   Compare, for example,
the rate of illegitimacy in the different counties
of which this district is composed.

SCOTLAND

AVERAGE NO. ILLEGITIMATE
In each 1000 Births
Ten Years, 1876-85.

REGISTRATION GROUPS OF
COUNTIES.

Below 75
75—100
100—125 NONE
125—150

NORTHERN
77

NORTH WESTERN
64

EAST MIDLAND
69

WEST MIDLAND
65

SOUTH EASTERN
78

SOUTH WESTERN
88

7   Longitude West 6   of Greenwich   5   4   3

TABLE XIV.—To 1,000 Births in each of the following Counties in North-Eastern Scotland,
how many were Illegitimate?

Scotland, N.-E. District.	1858.	Average of Ten Years, 1876–1885.	1886.	1887.	1893.
Aberdeen	158	137	142	135	
Banff	160	164	162	165	
Elgin	116	153	149	149	
Nairn	89	106	146	94	
Kincardine	130	125	123	124	
Average of all the above	146	141	144	137	

Little or no amelioration in its tendency
toward illicit relationships has taken place in
these counties since the facts were first discovered. One in seven,—that was its tribute
to bastardy in 1858, and that tribute it pays
to-day. It seem to me that the most plausible
explanation of this remarkable local proclivity
toward immorality is, that it is primarily due to
ancestral tendencies, coming, it may be, from
pre-historic times. Probably the immediate
and active cause to-day is the contagion of
loose example, the near inheritance of unwise
proclivity. The subject of illegitimacy in Scotland deserves a special study, occurring as it

does in a country distinguished above every other in Europe [1] by its zeal for orthodox belief.

Evidence of hereditary proclivity in this respect is not wanting in other lands. The islands of the Pacific have for the most part become converted to Christianity ; but travellers do not report the existence among the islanders of any very rigid rules of chastity. The negro, transplanted from his native barbarism to America, Christianized, educated, and given the rights and privileges of citizenship, retains as a race, it would seem, nearly all the vicious and lascivious propensities of his forefathers in the jungles of Africa. The rate of illegitimacy prevailing in the American capital is three times that of London ; but this is almost entirely due to the coloured population.

Where statistics are so absolutely wanting as in most parts of America it is not satisfactory to make deductions,[2] yet the opinion of those

---

[1] Those interested in the geographical distribution of illegitimacy will find in the Appendix several tables of interest, not elsewhere to be found out of Official Reports.

[2] Writing in 1845, Sir G. Graham, the Registrar General, said : " The United States in respect to Statistics of health

who have studied the condition of the Free
South is decidedly unfavourable to the standard
of female chastity which prevails among the
coloured population throughout the Southern
States,—even after nearly thirty years of emancipation and the rights of free citizenship.
Everywhere the same story can be read,
wherever different races are living under one
flag. Sicilian and Lombard are Italians, Bre-
ton and Norman are French, but there is some-
far deeper than the bond of a common language,
or a mutual attachment to the same form of
government. Indeed I know of few studies
of more absorbing interest than the tracing
out through the statistics of vice and crime, of
insanity and suicide, the workings of destiny
through natural laws, and the influence of
ancestral vices and virtues upon character and
conduct in humanity to-day.

A few other points deserve passing mention,

---

and human life is on nearly the same footing as Asia and
Africa." This criticism is at present not quite fair ; for as
regards Japan, there are better vital statistics obtainable
to-day than for the United States of America, where the
only record of vital statistics for the entire country is made
but once in ten years.

F

although they are of more interest to the student of moral pathology than to the general reader.

1. *At what age are young women most apt to fall into relations which make illegitimate births possible?*

Only two countries—Denmark and Sweden —afford any facilities for a scientific reply to this question. It is unlikely that their experience corresponds precisely with that of other nations; and certainly the reply they afford is quite contrary to what we should expect.

TABLE XV.—TO 1,000 UNMARRIED WOMEN AT EACH PERIOD OF LIFE, HOW MANY ILLEGITIMATE CHILD-BIRTHS PER YEAR?

Country.	Age of the mothers at birth of the illegitimate children.							
	15—	20—	25—	30—	35—	40—	45—	All ages together.
SWEDEN. Towns	7	51	71	62	41	17	1	39
,, Rural Districts	3	26	41	39	29	13	1	19
DENMARK. Towns[1]	6	33	52	47	31	14	1	27
,, Rural Districts	6	39	58	47	33	15	1	29

[1] Exclusive of Copenhagen.

It will be seen at once that, so far as Denmark and Sweden are concerned, the greatest liability for such births is not early in the life of unmarried womanhood ; but between twenty-five and thirty-five years. Even after the age of forty it is higher than under twenty! But these figures are insufficient for any safe deductions as regards other countries of Europe ; for while it is possible that elsewhere there obtains this same phenomenon of increased illegitimacy with increased age of women, we know nothing for certain. These figures are, perhaps, liable to misconstruction in another respect, for they include the illegitimate children of widows and unmarried women in middle life. What it would be very desirable to ascertain, is the age of girl-mothers when they give birth to the first illegitimate child. We should then know to what extent the greater evil exists ; but this information is not yet anywhere obtainable.

2. *From what class do they chiefly come ?*

Here, too, the facts are very meagre, consisting of a single inquiry for a single year, in Scotland. In 1883, the occupations of the 10,010 mothers of illegitimate children were by the Registrar General tabulated as follows :—

Domestic servants	4706
Girls working in factories. . . .	2442
„ „ on farms	985
Seamstresses	607
No occupation (chiefly daughters of working men)	831
Daughters of professional men . . .	54
No information (chiefly widows) . .	385

———————

10,010

3. *To what extent is concealment successful?*

This is a question, of course, impossible to answer by statistics, since naturally they cannot account for what is obviously concealed. It seems to be the general impression among physicians, best qualified to know, that, among classes able and willing to afford some expense rather than undergo disgrace, absolute concealment is of very ordinary occurrence. This, of course, does not apply to the lowest strata of population. " No one," says the author of " John Halifax, Gentleman," " can have taken any interest in the working classes without being aware how frightfully common among them is what they term 'a misfortune'; how few young women come to the marriage altar at all; or come just a week or two before maternity." But if this statement be true it must apply only to that lowest grade of society from whom the sense of shame has nearly departed. A little higher class of girls are pushed by their " misfortune " to the streets, there to swell, at least for a time, the ranks of prostitution. In the upper middle classes of society, misfortunes of this kind are doubtless very rare in comparison with others ; but they are readily concealed ; indeed, it is possible that the great majority of girl-mothers of the middle ranks not merely hide their fall, but ultimately marry persons who have no idea of their previous misstep. The character of Lady Dedlock is not unknown outside the pages of fiction. Even Lord Nelson carried to his grave the delusion that the mother of his " little Horatia " had borne no other children ; and Sir William Hamilton died believing in the fidelity of his wife.

The evils resulting from illegitimacy as a phase of the social problem are for the most part evident enough. Perhaps it may be doubted whether in Christian lands the un-happiness it occasions can be equalled by any other deviation from rectitude. Far more serious than disgrace is that saddest crime of humanity, the infanticide to which it so often leads. It is only now and then that the veil is drawn, and we get full glimpses of the truth; but everywhere we are confronted with the facts that, even in Christian England, the chance of living for the illegitimate child is far less than for others. In 1875 the Registrar General pointed out that while the death rate of legitimate children during the first year of life was about 205 per thousand, that of illegitimate was more than twice as great, or 418 per thousand births. Some of the worst discre-

TABLE XVI.—To 1,000 INFANTS BORN OF EACH CLASS, HOW MANY DIED UNDER ONE YEAR? (1875).

Towns.	Legitimate	Illegitimate.
Preston	214	448
Liverpool	205	418
Nottingham	191	365
Radford	187	547
Driffield	168	596

NOTE.—" During a long series of years it was found, in one part of Copenhagen (Denmark), that of illegitimate children, 45 per cent. of the boys, and 40 per cent. of girls, died before the age of one year, while the corresponding numbers for legitimate children were 20 and 18.—Dr. Sörensen, " Infant Mortality in Denmark."

pancies between the chances for life of the two classes, are seen in the foregoing table.

Even in rural districts where the general mortality among infants was low, the same wide divergence was found between the two classes. In twelve districts with a specially low rate it was found that the proportion of children dying during the first year of infancy was 97 per thousand for legitimate, and 293 per thousand for the illegitimate. Even in Stratford-upon-Avon, the death rate for the one class was but 69 per thousand, against a rate of 239 per thousand for children of unmarried mothers! In Glasgow, observations extending over three years (1873–75) show that while the mortality of legitimate children fluctuated between 149 and 154 per thousand, under one year of age, the corresponding mortality of the illegitimate was between 277 and 293 per thousand, or nearly twice as much.

How much of this mortality is due to deliberation and design? How much to that criminal indifference and neglect which eludes detection and escapes punishment? We have it on high authority that in civilized England there are parents who will suffer their legitimate

children to be starved to death for the sake of
a few shillings insurance head-money. What
chance then has the babe to live who, never
welcome, was put out to a professional baby-
farmer? Hardly a month goes by without
some awful story of this kind coming to
light; and yet how many of these baby-
murderers escape detection, and go on with
their work! Coroners are justly suspicious of
those frequent "accidents" to which these
unfortunate and unwelcome infants seem so
singularly liable. From the Judicial Reports
of England and Wales I have extracted the
number of coroner's inquests held during six
years, simply upon illegitimate children under
one year of age.

	1882.	1883.	1884.	1885.	1886.	1887.	Total Six Years.
Boys . . .	482	498	560	583	541	555	3219
Girls . . .	428	449	481	438	534	488	2818
Both sexes .	910	947	1041	1021	1075	1043	6037

These figures are sad enough when we know
what they mean. What is the nature of these
"accidents"? The Registrar General tells us

how these children die. They are suffocated, drowned, poisoned, strangled, scalded, burned alive. Yet these, perhaps, are more merciful exits than the induced disease, the slow starvation, the prolonged agony which many must undergo before finally released. Of these deaths by "misadventure," Dr. Acton says that the great majority, we are justified in assuming, "were the illegitimate offspring of first falls from virtue. The hopeless difficulty of rearing her offspring, the maddening'misery and want, have, in most of these cases, caused the mother to raise her hand against the life 'she has given." This was written before complete statistics were available ; but although we now see that the majority of coroner's inquests are not held upon illegitimate children, yet, in proportion to their number living, these are every year *more than four times as liable to " accidents " as their legitimate kindred.* Is there any explanation or reason for this ? One, only. These are not all accidents. They are undetected and unpunished murders of unwelcome guests at the feast of life.

Nevertheless, regarding illegitimacy for a moment as a phase of social phenomena, but quite independently of its ethical relations, is it possible to discover in it any effect for good ? I think we must admit, so considering it, that like other forms of generally deleterious action, such as War and Pain, even in this way, at the cost of individual happiness, Nature sometimes accomplishes a gain for humanity at large. It tends for one thing to level upward the human race. In the vast majority of cases·of illegitimacy, the mother is the inferior of the two parents, not merely in social rank, but often in that fineness of mental and physical organization which results from better conditioned lines of ancestry. Thus, when two races are brought after the violence of conquest into relations with each other, and begin, the conquerors and the conquered, to blend into a single nationality, it is rather concubinage than marriage which breaks down the first barriers of prejudice. The tendency of legal unions is almost always upon a plane of equality; Cinderella we find in the fairy tales for children, but in real life it is Emma Lyons and Nelly Gwynn whom for the most part history shows us in her place. Of that fusion of Celt and Roman, Saxon, Dane, and Norman into the English people,

how much was due at the outset to relations
unsanctioned by Church or State ? Why, even
within the present generation we were told by
Sir George Graham, the late Registrar General,
that " if the mortality were not greater among
illegitimate than among legitimate children,
every fifteenth person in England must be of
illegitimate extraction." [1] But this is merely
the story of to-day. Begin to trace ancestry
backward, and it is probable that in one branch
or another, the bar-sinister would be found
somewhere in the ancestral pedigree by more
than half the general population of Great
Britain, and by three-fourths of its aristocracy,
before one reaches the period of the Reforma-
tion. Now so far as the English stock is
improved in physical and mental calibre by
infusion of better blood, just so far some benefit
accrues to the race, even though it be at the
cost of individual happiness and honour.

Everywhere the same phenomena are to be
seen. In certain parts of America the aboriginal tribes are disappearing—not always by
fire and sword, but through absorption into the

---

[1] Sixth Annual Report of Registrar General, p. 38.

conquering race ; and in more than one American to-day, the blood of the *Mayflower* Puritans runs, in commingled currents, with that of the aboriginal tribes they dispossessed. One cannot travel through the States without noting that the thick lips, coal-black colour, low brow, and flat nose of the Guinea negro have almost disappeared in a hybrid race, with large admixture of English blood—changing not only the colour, but the intellectual capacity of the type ; and I do not doubt that before half-a-dozen centuries have expired, the African will have as completely merged his race in the three hundred millions of the North American Continent, as Phenician and Greek, Saracen, Roman and Norman have blended in the Neapolitan who basks in the sunshine on San Lucia. The New Zealand traveller a thousand years hence, who from his reverie above the ruins of London Bridge turns his step homeward through the Gulf States of America, will find no negroes ; but the labouring class of the population, the hewers of wood and the drawers of water, will no doubt show a warmer tint than obtains in what now is Canada and the Northern States. Yet I question whether this tawny population will more widely differ from the general mass, than the Sicilian or Calabrian differ from the nations of Lombardy, or the type of Grenada from that of Castile. Of course the greater part of this change is henceforth to be effected by lawful marriage, but the barriers between races are at first otherwise broken down; and this was no exception. The United States minister to Hayti is the son of a slaveholder and his slave.[1]

Nor can we deny the gain to humanity which here and there nature grants in individual cases,

---

[1] At the International Congress of Hygiene and Demography held in London in August, 1891, Dr. Carlsen of Copenhagen presented a pamphlet showing certain statistical investigations concerning the idiots and feeble-minded portion of the Danish population.

" The illegitimate imbecile children amounted to 5 per cent. of the total number of imbeciles, while about 10 per cent. of all births have been illegitimate in Denmark during a long period of time. As it is probable that the number of the imbeciles overlooked or forgotten in the counting is larger within the class of legitimate than within that of illegitimate children, we incline to the supposition (even if proper attention is paid to the fact of the greater ráte of mortality for illegitimate children) *that imbecility is scarcer among illegitimate than among legitimate children ;* which accords very well with the fact, that the more malignant forms of imbecility *occur less frequently among the illegitimate children.*"

while still exacting her tribute of personal suffering. The world could ill spare all upon the accident of whose birth it puts a social stigma. Some of the greatest soldiers and adventurers of ancient and modern times, from William the Conqueror of England to Pizarro the Conqueror of Peru; from Marechal de Saxe to General Burgoyne—not to speak of a greater than them all, in our own time—might have borne the *bar sinister* upon their escutcheon. The most brilliant name in French journalism for forty years, Emile de Girardin, gained his position in literature by his genius, despite an openly acknowledged illegitimate origin. There died in France a few years ago an ecclesiastic than whom few more eloquent or far-sighted has the nation ever known; upon whom the Church conferred its highest honour, whom the French Academy raised to a seat among its Immortals; yet the Bishop of Orleans was the son of a maid-servant at a Swiss inn, and knew no father. Who that visits Washington, the American capital, suspects that the only National Museum of the great Republic, the " Smithsonian Institution," founded " for the increase and diffusion of knowledge among men,"

was the generous gift, more than half a century
ago, to a nation then insignificant in numbers,
from the natural son of an English duke?
When, a century ago, the American colonies
had emerged from their conflict with the
mother-country, it was chiefly the genius of one
man who laid the foundation of that federal
system, which, by a written constitution,
moulded these discordant and petty States into
the potentiality of a mighty nation; but
Alexander Hamilton was of illegitimate birth,
the son of a Scotch planter in the West Indies.
One of the two greatest names in modern
American history confessed his belief that
whatever talent he possessed came to him
through a parent whose birth was illegitimate.
Philosophy, profiting by the studies of D'Alem-
bert, one of the keenest mathematicians and
most brilliant writers of the last century, does
not identify the philosopher, honoured by the
courts of Catherine II. and Frederic the Great,
and by the Vatican itself, with a poor foundling
picked up in the gutters of Paris. Literature
forgets the stain of ignoble origin in Boccaccio,
the father of Italian prose; in Erasmus of
Rotterdam, the greatest name in the history of

the Renaissance ; in George Sand, great grand-child of Maurice de Saxe, himself the natural son to Augustus, King of Saxony, or in Alexander Dumas of to-day, illegitimate son of a still more renowned father, who was grandson of a French marquis and a slave-woman of San Domingo. Who that stands in the refectory of the Dominican Convent at Milan before the fading outlines of that matchless masterpiece— The Last Supper—remembers the story of Leonardo di Vinci's birth ? Who that reads the story of Pharez connects him with the history of David ?

What of prevention ? Here is a social evil growing out of laxity of life, but it is an evil of which the heaviest penalty falls upon those least to blame. Something indeed may be hoped from the strengthening of religious influences, and the inculcation of a greater sense of responsibility, or by modification of laws and customs which directly or injuriously hinder early marriages. Unfortunately, the truth is, that everything which makes for early and improvident marriages tends to repress illegitimacy ; while all prudential restraints, whether imposed by law or custom, tend to its increase. One good thing is certain, that in England there has been a steady fall, in the rate of illegitimacy since the year 1845. In that year the rate was 70 per thousand births. In 1889 the proportion was 46.

Is it not possible to ameliorate in some measure the awful evils which spring from it? Without in any degree lessening for young men the obligation to chaste and sober lives, might it not be possible to suggest also the truth that paternity, even outside the law, creates duties which no honourable man will ever seek to evade? For no child meets with death from the hands of her whose breast should have been its safest refuge, or, abandoned to its fate, is slowly tortured out of existence in the filthy attic of a " baby-farm," except from the neglected secondary duty of some man. The performance of such parental obligations may not indeed atone for the primary fault; but that fault is infinitely increased by its neglect. It needs to be affirmed that honour creates responsibilities which the law may not enforce; that parentage implies duty; that the natural right of illegitimate infancy to paternal support depends in no way upon legal claims or good-natured generosity, but upon the foundation principles of justice and right.

And finally it seems to me very questionable whether that essentially feminine sentiment which affixes upon illegitimate motherhood of a young girl the stigma of irreparable infamy, does not, in the majority of cases, accomplish more evil than good. It may be well to teach innocence the exceeding sinfulness of sin; yet even here there is a tendency to evil consequences just so far as we overstep exact truth. To assert that by maternity out of marriage, the character and nature of a young girl is infected with pollution; that if a housemaid she is henceforth unfit to care for children, and for the sake of example and in the name of Virtue, should be turned forthwith, and without warning, upon the streets, as the pitiless law of England to-day permits,—this is not merely false, but the underlying sentiment that inspires such action is both inexpedient and unjust. Is it maternity that destroys the purity of womanhood, or the lapse which precedes maternity? For one, I refuse to believe that we ever can make virtue seem more lovely by the merciless punishment of that consequence, which alone more than half condones the sin. I very seriously question whether every seventh mother in some counties of Scotland is worthy of that stigma of dishonour which belongs to her only who sells herself for hire.

Nor is it expedient, because whenever the extreme penalty of ostracism is mercilessly inflicted, we create a yet greater evil than the one it is sought to condemn. Between that first child of the young country girl, and those depths of sin, to which the painted hetaire of the pavement has fallen, is an almost im-measurable abyss. Yet it needs but a step to reach that lower level ; a step over a precipice. That Christian woman who, deaf to all en-treaty, turns her maid into the streets because about to become a mother, may fancy she is only upholding the dignity of virtue ; but she is also opening to her sister woman the gates of hell. She has created that despair which pushes its victims into a chasm, wherein thousands of her sisters annually fall. Prosti-tution is the final resource of illegitimate mater-nity ; and more than one Fantine sells her soul on the streets of London to keep her child alive.

But even this is not the lowest depth. She who pushes her sister towards despair helps to create in her soul the temptation to escape all ignominy by infanticide. We do not need the genius of Scott, of Goethe, of George Eliot to tell us that in our Christian civilization a mother can do, what the old Hebrew thought almost impossible, " forget her sucking child." Even the criminal records give us but a hint of the awful evil that in reality exists. There is no danger more terrible than this ; for in the soul of a woman who has lost the instinct of maternal love there is indeed a ruin beyond repair.

I hope it may not be wholly an idle dream that, at some period in the development of Christian charity and civilization, a point may be reached where she who is about to become a mother of an unwelcome child, because she trusted too faithfully and loved too well, will find somewhere a sure refuge ; meeting there neither a blind sympathy that hastens too quickly to condone, nor yet an unpitying virtue that scorns forgiveness and invites to despair. In her sad extremity, perchance then she may be encouraged by woman's heart and helped

by womanly hands not to evade the responsibilities of motherhood, but to meet them so
bravely, to fulfil them so conscientiously, that
in time even the stain of her dishonour shall
fade away, and her transgressions, through duty
well performed, find forgiveness and expiation.

CONCLUSIONS.

I Illegitimacy is a phase of social phenomena produced by the conjoint action of several
causes.   Its variance in different localities
depends upon the force and number of the
factors there present.

II. These causes differ in energy; they
sometimes neutralize each other ; but on the
whole, with certain exceptions, hereafter noted,
the rate of illegitimacy fairly expresses their
effect upon the private sentiment of the community concerned.

III. In all sections of the United Kingdom
it is chiefly prevalent where thrift and prosperity are most general, and is least in that
country where poverty is the ordinary condition of the mass of the people.

IV. In Great Britain it seems to prevail least

among the population of cities, and chiefly in rural communities.

V. Among the nations of Europe it is most common where elementary education is most generally diffused ; and least among some of the most illiterate communities, as in Brittany and Ireland.

VI. It is probably increased by any restraint on early marriage, whether imposed by law, or custom, or arising from severe industrial depression.

VII. The influence of religion is one of the most powerful agencies against unchastity ; but the effect upon illegitimacy of a religious creed apparently has no relation to its dogmatic truth.

VIII. Differences in the annual prevalence of illegitimacy in different localities or sections of the same country are so marked, and so persistent, that only by the hypothesis of hereditary influence can we at present account for them.

IX. As a means for testing the comparative sensitiveness of different people to moral laws, the rate of illegitimacy can only serve when the totality of general environment is similar, as between cities or communities under the same general government. We cannot always infer the existence of a higher tone of morals from a low rate of illegitimate births (1) in countries where ante-natal destruction of life largely prevails ; (2) in countries where young women are specially guarded before marriage, yet wherein marital fidelity may be less observed ; (3) in countries wherein polyandry is alleged to exist as an acknowledged custom ; or (4) in great cities where other vices counteract tendency to this, and where opportunities for concealment are far greater than in country districts.

X. While the rate of illegitimacy is widely different in each of the three divisions of the United Kingdom, it is evident that in each it has been slowly declining for many years. It appears also to be decreasing in frequency in the greater part of Europe, at least when measured by the rate prevalent twenty years ago.

THE INFLUENCE OF SEASONS
UPON CONDUCT.

In the "Journal of Marie Bashkirtseff," that
book without a parallel, that "exhibition of an
imposing tapestry in reverse," as Mr. Gladstone
has so aptly called it, there occurs a passage
wherein the young girl-artist attempts to de-
scribe her ideal of a painting, upon which she
was unconsciously putting the last enthusiastic
labour of her fading life. It was an endeavour,
as her biographer tells us, to express the in-
most spirit of Springtime by line and colour;
all that mysterious fermentation which accom-
panies the reviving year. "I go to Sevres
every day; this picture possesses me," she
writes in her journal. "The apple-tree is in
blossom; the leaves beginning to come out,
there are violets in the grass. The air is
balmy, and the girl who dreams, leaning against
the tree, is 'languishing and intoxicated.' . . .

It would be fine if I succeeded in rendering the effect of sap in the spring! . . . I want a real big goose of a girl, who dreams, overcome by the heat, and who will yield to the first peasant who chances to go by."

If there is in this passage a realism of expression a little foreign to our general usage, it betrays notwithstanding that curious gift of insight within the very heart of Nature, which Marie Bashkirtseff possessed. For she touched here a mystery of profound significance. Art and poetry have long affirmed the emotional tendencies which accompany the budding year : we know by heart Tennyson's oft-quoted lines. Now beyond fanciful but vague sentiment, is it possible to penetrate to the truth, and to discover in so distant and abstract a circumstance as the season of the year, any periodical and distinct incitement toward human actions? One is inclined, at first thought, to relegate such an inquiry to other ages, when planets decided destiny, and the stars in their courses fought against Sisera. But this question to-day commands somewhat greater respect than is due the dreams of astrology. It is a scientific problem, because facts are observed, which are explicable on no other hypothesis than a disturbance of equilibrium, so to speak, which so regularly recurs, year after year, as to denote the activity of some law of causation.

It is not a new theory, though I propose to carry it somewhat further than it has been pushed hitherto. Over half a century ago, Quetelet in his great work " On Man," suggested the hypothesis, although he deplored the want of statistical evidence which alone hindered verification of strong probabilities. To-day we are far better situated, so far as concerns opportunity for the observation of phenomena of human action in abnormal directions. The hypothesis toward which all the facts point is simply this ; that upon the nervous organization of human bodies (perhaps specially upon dwellers in the temperate zones) there is exerted during the procession of the seasons, from winter's close till midsummer, some undefined, specific influence, which in some manner tends to increase the excitability of emotion and passion, and thus also to increase all actions arising therefrom. How this is accomplished is another problem, of which more hereafter. Naturally too, we can see but a very limited portion of the field of human conduct; for only those actions which are so serious as to call for legal or medical investigation can be subject to scientific observation. If, however, there be any truth in the hypothesis we should expect these when studied *en masse* to be uniformly more frequent at certain periods of the year than at others. Are they? What are the facts?

There are six phases of human conduct in regard to which I believe the action of this cosmic force may be recognised. These are :—

I. Suicide, accomplished or attempted.

II. Crimes against Persons.

III. Murder and Homicidal Assaults.

IV. Crimes against Chastity.

V. Attacks of Insanity.

VI. Births, especially the illegitimate births.

Besides these there are one or two others, upon which some light glimmers, but as yet not clearly.

I. *Suicide.*—Whether or not we assume self-destruction as the evidence of unsound mind, it is certain that nearly always it results from a temporarily distorted estimate of the value of

further existence.   A man may apparently be
sane enough on every other topic ; it is only
about himself or some conditions of personal
environment that his ideas are unbalanced.

For a long time, suicide was supposed to
find its culmination of frequency, particularly in
England, at that season of gloom when poverty
and distress are most keenly felt.   But this
notion has been ruthlessly swept away by the
evidence of statistics.   Nothing apparently is
more clearly proven than that the tendency to
suicide in every country in Europe regularly
increases from the end of winter until July,
and then slowly declines.   Morselli has shown
that the point of greatest aptitude toward
suicide during the periods observed was
reached, for Ireland, Saxony, Austria, Sweden,
and Holland in *May* ; for France, Italy, Russia,
Norway, Belgium, and Denmark, in *June* ; and
for Switzerland and one or two divisions of
the German Empire as late even as *July*.   For
the majority of dwellers in Europe the greatest
extreme of tendency towards suicide will, I
think, some day be discovered to be a period
of about five weeks in May and June.   On the
other hand, *without exception*, that period of

the year when the suicidal impulse is *least* felt
occurs during winter when cold, hunger, and
destitution are generally most severely felt.

We may see the facts clearly, if we divide
the year into two parts and calculate the proportion of suicides which in different countries
occur in each half year; and this I have done
in the final table.

But the operation of this law is not confined
to Europe alone; and in the statistics of the
extreme Orient, I have recently found a remarkable coincidence of the same phenomenon.

TABLE I.—PROPORTION OF SUICIDES IN EACH SEASON OF THE
YEAR TO THE TOTAL NUMBER.—JAPANESE EMPIRE.

SEASONS.	1882.	1883.	1884.	1885.	Average 4 years.
SPRING—March, April, May	28	28	27	27	27·4
SUMMER—June, July, August	30	29	29	32	30
AUTUMN—September, October, November .	23	22	22	23	22·6
WINTER—December, January, February .	19	21	22	18	20
Total Year .	100	100	100	100	100

If we take the suicides of the Japanese Empire
for several successive years, it will be found
that they recur in each season of the year in
almost the same proportion as in Western
Europe.

Thus, year after year, in Eastern Asia, between 57 and 59 per cent. of all suicides occur
in the two seasons between the 1st of March
and the last of August.

How is it with ourselves ?   Unfortunately
the data furnished by the Registrar General,
except for London, tell us nothing of the season
of suicide in England and Wales.   It so happens, however, that some knowledge is obtainable from another quarter.   When the would-be
suicide fails in the attempt at self-destruction
the act becomes a crime to be noted by the
Police, and accounted for in the Judicial Reports, where criminal returns are made for each
quarter of the year.   These cases of attempted
suicide, numbering about a thousand a year
(10,733 for ten years, 1878–87), probably represent only a small part of those which actually occur ; since of course in a private family
of means, the act would be treated by physicians
and friends as merely an incident to the delirium

of a disordered mind. It is different, however, when a girl flings herself over London Bridge, or a man shoots himself in Whitechapel. Now if we divide the last ten years for which the Judicial Reports afford the facts, into three periods, we shall see how exactly the intensity of suicide-tendency in this country agrees with the accession of spring and summer, and how uniformly it decreases during the colder seasons.

TABLE II.—OF ATTEMPTS AT SUICIDE IN ENGLAND AND WALES DURING TEN YEARS, WHAT PER CENT. OCCURRED DURING EACH QUARTER OF THE YEAR?

Quarters of the Year.	1878–1880.	1881–1883.	1884–1887.	Average for 10 years.
April, May, June .	28	29	29	28·8
July, Aug., Sep. .	32	30	32	31·6
Oct., Nov., Dec. .	21	22	19	20·3
Jan., Feb., March. .	19	19	20	19·3
	100	100	100	100·0

In England and Wales, therefore, fully sixty per cent. of all attempts at suicide occur during the warmer seasons, and forty per cent. during autumn and winter. See how closely these proportions agree with those of Japan!

For the metropolis we are able to get nearer to the truth regarding the act of suicide itself. In a paper read before the Royal Statistical Society in February 1886, Dr. W. Ogle has calculated the average monthly distribution of all suicides in London during a period of twenty years, 1865–1884. In each thousand cases of self-destruction annually occurring the proportion for each season is found to be as follows:—

SPRING : March, April, May	278	} 56%
SUMMER : June, July, August	282	
AUTUMN : September, October, November	226	} 44%
WINTER : December, January, February	214	

1000

Notwithstanding the fact that distress among the London poor is far greater in winter than at any other season,—suicide then is least prevalent, and most frequent in May and June.

Does this suicidal tendency manifest itself uniformly year after year ? It does. If we construct a diagram from the exact numbers of attempts at suicide in England, during each quarter, extending it over a continuous period of several years, we can clearly see how this wave of impulse sweeps over us.

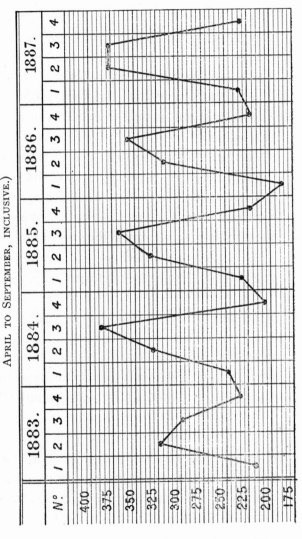

England and Wales. Curve Diagram showing Attempts at Suicide, during each Quarter of the Years 1883–1887. (The second and third Quarters are the months April to September, inclusive.)

H

Looking at such a diagram, the physician can hardly fail to note its resemblance to the tracing of a pulse, or the rise and fall of temperature during progress of a fever. It may be that such resemblance is even more than a fancy, and that suicide thus marks in truth the variations of the fever of life. At all events there can be no doubt whatever of the periodicity of change, regularly coincident with the advent of the opening year. Everywhere in northern climes the number of voluntary deaths steadily increases from the beginning of the year until May, June, or July, and then as regularly and uniformly declines.

II. *Insanity.*—Why is it that at certain and fixed periods in the cycle of the year, a sort of tidal wave of mental aberration regularly sweeps over civilized mankind? Wherever the facts are investigated it is found that with the advent of spring, and extending into the summer, there is invariably an increase in lunacy. For a long time it has been noted by those in medical charge of asylums for the insane, that as spring advances an increase in excitement, a peculiar mental restlessness, seems to affect the patients; but facts of this nature have not thus far as-

sumed any statistical expression. In the admission of patients attacked with insanity to
asylums and retreats, we are face to face with
evidence upon which we can depend.

This phenomenal increase of mental excitement or depression has also been noted for many
years. Quetelet refers to the admissions into
the great Insane Asylum at Charenton near
Paris, of which 54 per cent. were received
between the 1st of March and the 1st of September. Drs. Bucknill and Tuke quote similar
figures (but without date) which by calculation
produce the same proportion, and show that 54
per cent. of admissions to asylums occur during
the warmer months. But I have more recent
evidence. In the last report of Dr. Ritti, the
physician in charge of the female wards at
Charenton, he gives the number of admissions
for the years from 1879 to 1888. Of these 53
per cent. are during the period between March
and August, and 47 per cent. between September and the following February. " During
the last ten years," writes Dr. Ritti, " it is in
spring-time that the admissions have become
the most numerous ; they have slightly di-
minished during summer, and reached their

minimum during the last months of the year."

But by far the most complete and interesting of recent statistics on this subject that I have been able to find, are contained in the Lunacy Reports of Scotland. Here for two different periods, of not less than eighteen years altogether, the admission to asylums may be seen for each month; and as the total number of the insane thus accounted for is over 38,000, the averages thus obtained undoubtedly represent, with exceptional accuracy, the working of the law. And every year the story is substantially the same. Commencing about the month of March, the number of admissions to retreats and asylums begins to rise above the average of the year, and gradually attaining its maximum during the early part of the summer, falls below the average in September, and remains below during the autumn and winter, only to rise again with the advent of the season of fertilization.

In other words, certain forms of insanity are coincident with the impulse to suicide, subject alike to an increasing prevalence with the coming of spring.

TABLE III.—OF EACH 1,000 ADMISSIONS TO INSANE
ASYLUMS IN SCOTLAND DURING THE PERIODS
NAMED, HOW MANY OCCURRED DURING DIFFERENT
SEASONS?

Seasons.	Men.		Women.	
	1865–74 10 years.	1880–87 8 years.	1865–74 10 years.	1880–87 8 years.
Spring and Summer.	527	529	533	538
Autumn and Winter.	473	471	467	462
Total being	1,000	1,000	1,000	1,000

Both sexes are apparently susceptible to this
mysterious influence, although in slightly different proportions. But whether for men or for
women, for one period or another, or for single
years, about 53 per cent. of all persons attacked
with insanity in Scotland are admitted to
asylums and retreats during the six months
following the 1st of March. There can be no
dispute about facts so susceptible of proof, so
recurrent every year. The precise figures for

each month of the year will be found of interest to the student, and are given elsewhere.[1]

The remarkable correspondence between the varying proclivity to attacks of insanity and the tendency towards self-destruction has not failed to attract notice.

If upon the same scale we trace a diagram which for successive months shall indicate the proportionate percentage of attacks of insanity, almost exactly the same curve will be taken by suicide, except that the influence of spring is far more intense toward self-destruction. In regularity of course upward till midsummer, and downward during the remainder of the year, the line of perturbation is almost exactly the same. Both are nearly at their lowest degree of frequency when the year begins ; both rise with advancing spring ; both culminate at the same period, and decline with the dying year. This coincidence has led some writers to insist on the greater frequency of suicide in summer by reason of its relation to mental disease. The hypothesis is a plausible one ; some connection undoubtedly exists between

---

[1] See Table in Appendix.

them, but I question whether it be that of
cause and effect. It so happens, as Morselli
has pointed out, that whenever a distinction is
made between cases of self-destruction occurring
during an insane attack, and those due to other
causes, *precisely the same phenomenon is seen in
both instances ;* the highest rate of frequency is
found in spring and summer.

TABLE IV.—OF SUICIDES DUE TO MADNESS OR TO OTHER
CAUSES, WHAT PROPORTION OCCURRED DURING EACH
HALF-YEAR ?

	Suicides due to Insanity.			Suicides due to other causes.		
	Italy.	France.	Belgium.	Italy.	France.	Belgium.
Spring and Summer .	64·4	58·9	56·3	59·0	56·7	57·1
Autumn and Winter .	35·6	41·1	43·7	41·0	43·3	42·9
The year being . .	100·0	100·0	100·0	100·0	100·0	100·0

The inference is clear, for unless we ascribe
all suicide to madness, it is impossible to explain its variation by season on the theory of
insanity. Even then, we but push the problem
a little backward; what produces the suicidal
insanity ? It seems to me that we must look
for some influence which is common to both

phenomena, as an exciting or predisposing cause of each.

III. *Crimes of Violence.*—All actions are criminal which are in violation of the law. A crime is not necessarily morally wrong; it may be on the contrary a very noble and meritorious protest against injustice and tyranny, and yet by the laws of the country be punishable even with death.

Putting aside all minor subdivisions, crimes in every country, whether civilized or barbarous, may be divided into two great classes : infringments upon rights of Property, or injuries to the Person.   The exciting causes which induce these two kinds of offence, are as a rule different.   In the predatory instinct of the habitual thief, or the sudden impulse of temptation in destitution, we see examples of those causes which provoke crimes against property. These impulses, coincident often with opportunity and temptation, are peculiar to no season or clime, except that they are more frequent and numerous when food is dear, and work difficult to obtain. In India, crimes against property are in almost exact coincidence with the failure of crops, or the abundance and cheapness of food.

Crimes against persons, on the other hand, manifestly arise from very different causes. In the majority of cases they are the outcome of powerful passions, which, suddenly excited, break down all the barriers of prudential self-control. Sudden anger, and resentment springing even from the most trifling disputes, desire for revenge of deeper injuries, real or imaginary, jealousy and rage, and other passions, common to brute and man,—all these may occasion assaults upon the person of the individual.

It is therefore in this class or species of crime that we may expect to detect the influence of seasons, if such influence exists.

Now the Judicial Reports of England and Wales fortunately afford us means of testing the problem, since we can tabulate year after year, all crimes against persons, so far as these offences were reported to the police authorities. If there be no effect upon criminal acts exerted by the variance of temperature and the change of season, we should find no correspondence to exist between them. Murderous assaults, for example, or crimes growing out of sex-passions, would be distributed over the entire year, with-

out preponderance at any season ; or manifest-
ing a preponderance, sometimes in winter, and
sometimes in spring. In the following table I
have grouped together in one class all assaults
affecting human life, excepting only the murder

TABLE V.—OF THE TOTAL NUMBER OF .MURDERS OR
MURDEROUS ASSAULTS IN ENGLAND AND WALES DURING
A PERIOD OF TEN YEARS, HOW MANY OCCURRED DURING
EACH OF THE FOUR QUARTERS OF THE YEAR?

	Total No. of Crimes.		Per cent. each quarter year.	
	1878–1882.	1883–1887.	1878–1882.	1883–1887.
1. Jan., Feb., March, .	412	451	21	23
2. April, May, June .	491	506	25	25
3. July, Aug., Sept. .	566	567	29	28
4. Oct., Nov., Dec. .	488	469	25	24
Total	1957	1993	100	100

of infants under one year. I do not suppose
that the inclusion of these would materially
change the result; but infanticide differs from
other acts of homicide in this respect, that it does
not spring from passionate rage or anger against
the victim, but is more frequently the outcome

of selfishness, of desire to avoid responsibility, or to escape shame. The preceding table includes all other cases of murder or manslaughter, and all reported attempts at homicide of every description in England and Wales for a period of ten years. Of the total number of such crimes in each of two periods, what per cent. occurred in each of the four quarters of the year?

It appears, therefore, that in England and Wales 53 or 54 per cent. of homicidal or murderous attacks occur during the period from April 1st to Sept. 30th, as against 46 or 47 per cent. during the colder months of the year. Or to put the figures in another and perhaps more intelligible form, we may say that during the ten years mentioned, 1878–1887, the number of murderous attacks occurred as follows :

    In Spring and Summer (April to Sept.) . 2128
    In Autumn and Winter (Oct. to March) . 1820

It is an excess of about three hundred homicides or attempted homicides during the warmer half of the year over and above what occur in autumn and winter. Probably, too, a certain number of murders owe their incitement to avarice and greed, rather than personal ani-

mosity; and these would be distributed throughout the year. If only those arising from passion
could be included, the proportionate difference
would undoubtedly be very much greater.

There is one species of crime more obviously
brutal than all others in its origin and character; I refer to assaults by force upon the
chastity of women and girls. The philosophic
student of the twenty-first century, contemplating the perplexing phases of social life in
an age which we sometimes fancy to be almost
the noon of civilization, will wonder how it
happened that in Christian England, until the
year 1885, a girl of fourteen years was deemed
incapable of entering into any legal contract
whatever, yet presumed to be perfectly capable
of tacitly assenting to her own ruin. Now I
have taken from the Judicial Reports the total
number of crimes springing from sex-passion, so
far as these were known to the police, during a
period of ten years. It is exceedingly probable
that many more crimes of this character were,
from various motives, concealed from the authorities; but these as given are sadly significant.
I have divided them into two periods of five
years each.

TABLE VI.—NUMBER OF CRIMES PERTAINING TO SEX-PASSION (RAPE, AND ASSAULTS AGAINST CHASTITY), IN ENGLAND AND WALES, DURING TEN YEARS, 1878–1887, AND THE PROPORTION COMMITTED EACH QUARTER OF THE YEAR.

	Total number of Crimes reported to Police.			What per cent. occurred during each Quarter ?		
	1878–82 5 years.	1883–87 5 years.	10 years.	1878–82	1883–87	10 years.
First Quarter: Jan., Feb., March .	611	866	1477	20	18	19
Second Quarter: April, May, June .	866	1359	2225	28	28	28
Third Quarter: July, Aug., Sept. .	987	1556	2543	32	32	32
Fourth Quarter: Oct., Nov., Dec. .	599	1053	1652	20	22	21
	3063	4834	7897	100	100	100

This table is of special interest. In no species of crime is the apparent effect of cosmic influence so evident as in offences of this kind. This is extremely significant.

It will be observed, of course, that the quarters of the year do not correspond with the seasons; but the divergence is not great. March is included with winter, and September goes with summer; but in all probability the influence of the first month of spring is stronger than the first month of autumn.

I have divided them into periods of five years, so that the reader may not only note how closely they correspond in proportional prevalence, but also that remarkable fact—*the great increase of crimes of this character* during recent years. In 1879 the total number of cases reported was 542. In 1887 the number had risen to 1,210, more than double. Yet there is no substantial change as regards the time of the year: whether for the first period or the last, it is just sixty per cent. of offences that apparently must needs come between the first of April and the last of Sept. A considerable part of this increased criminality was due to a change of the law. If it were true that we cannot make men virtuous by Act of Parliament, at least we can make them criminals; the law of the land to-day makes that a felony which for centuries of English history could not be legally punished. It is very curious to note the rise of crimes as the law begins to take effect.

The fluctuation of crimes of this character from season to season will be best seen by a diagram based upon the actual numbers for each quarter year. For example, during the first quarter of the year 1880, the total number of crimes of this kind was 140; the next quarter, from April to July, it rose to 180; from August to October, the third quarter, it remained at 182, rapidly falling during the colder season, and rising with the following spring.[1]

In France, too, the same correspondence between offences against chastity and the season of the year has been long noticed. In 1851, Dr. Villerme, in the Annals d'Hygiène, pointed out that a distribution of these crimes according to months discovered their especial frequency in May, June, and July. Later observations by Profs. Lacassagne and Tardieu, by Drs. Garraud and Bernard, confirm absolutely the earlier reports, and show that for France, as the last-named author states, " c'est en mai, juin, juillet et août que s'observe la plus grande frequence des attentats aux mœurs." [2] The curve from month to month through the year follows almost absolutely that taken by suicide and insanity, except that its

---

[1] From Tables in Appendix the reader can test the accuracy of this and other diagrams, by constructing them for himself. See diagram on the following page.

Arch. Anthropolog. Crim. 1886–7.

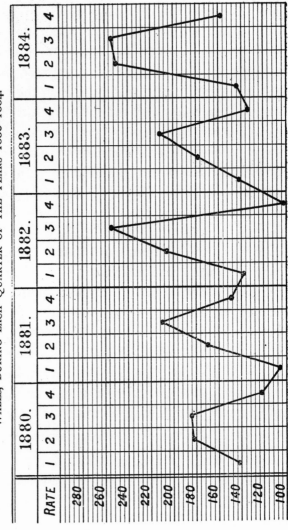

DIAGRAM SHOWING ACTUAL NUMBER OF CRIMES AGAINST CHASTITY, IN ENGLAND AND WALES, DURING EACH QUARTER OF THE YEARS 1880–1884.

rise and fall are more abrupt. Tardieu gives the figures for ten years 1860–69, showing no less than 63 per cent. of the whole number of such offences occurred during the six months April–October ; and almost the same result is shown by Bernard in his article to which I have referred.

IV. *All Crimes against the Person.*—The totality of "Crimes against Persons," exhibits the same phenomena, though in a less marked degree. It so happens that among crimes thus tabulated, there are some offences which perhaps are quite as frequently against the welfare of the commonwealth as against the individual. "Bigamy," for instance, or "child stealing"; "the abandonment of infants," or "concealment of their birth," are all tabulated in this country with "murder and manslaughter," as crimes against the person.

Taking, nevertheless, the total number of all crimes against persons, for ten years (1878–87), including not only those of the more serious kind just tabulated, but all others so far as known to the police, we find them to have been committed in months undermentioned in following proportions. As affording an interesting

I

comparison, I have brought together the same facts for Ireland, during the period of the years 1878–87, and for France during forty years, 1830–1869.

TABLE VII.—OF TOTAL CRIMES AGAINST THE PERSON, WHAT PER CENT. WERE COMMITTED DURING THE SEASONS SPECIFIED?

	Spring.	Summer.	Autumn.	Winter.	Year.
England 10 years, 1878–87	26	29	24	21	100
Ireland 10 years, 1878–87	25	28	24	23	100
France 40 years, 1830–69	28	27	22	23	100

Here, again, we find that all crimes, even those arising from personal antipathy or hatred, seem specially prevalent in the warmer half of the year. In England, 55 per cent. of all such acts of violence during the ten years 1878–1887 happened in spring and summer, and in France during a period of forty years the average was the same.[1] Ireland, indeed, shows a more

---

[1] The figures for France are taken from the "Compte-Gen. de la Justice Criminelle," p. cxvi. [1880]. See also Appendix.

even distribution of such crimes ; but the same tendency is seen even there.

V. *Birth-rates.*—The influence of season upon the birth-rate was suggested by Quetelet in 1824, who then pointed out that the number of children born in Belgium every year was always greatest about the months of January and February, a fact which supposes the maximum of conceptions in April and May. Now, among human beings is there yet remaining any trace of that instinct which leads birds to mate when winter goes, and which in earlier periods of man's development was perhaps as strong with him as with other animals ? If it exists, should we find any difference, in and out of the marriage relation ? The subject is so little known that I shall offer no apology for presenting whatever facts are obtainable.

On some accounts it is more satisfactory here to obtain proportions of each month or season to every 1,200 births occurring during the entire year ; since we then have a rate due each month of exactly 100 births, and can see at a glance whether in any given number of months we have more or less than the numbers due.

TABLE VIII.—OF EACH 1,200 LEGITIMATE BIRTHS ANNUALLY,
HOW MANY WERE THE RESULT OF CONCEPTIONS EACH
SEASON OF THE YEAR IN THE FOLLOWING COUNTRIES?

	France.	Norway.	Sweden.	Holland.	Italy.[1]
SPRING—Mar., April, May	310	315	313	321	318
SUMMER — June, July, August . .	314	309	307	310	315
AUTUMN—Sept.,Oct., Nov..	283	287	277	268	270
WINTER—December, Jan., Feb. . . .	293	289	303	301	297
The Year . .	1,200	1,200	1,200	1,200	1,200

Legitimate births therefore appear to be
slightly under the influence of seasons. The
difference in reproduction proclivity is not great,
but it is fairly suggestive of permanent influence.

More striking is the evidence of periodicity
in the proclivity to those relationships which
occasion illegitimate births. If in the earlier
stages of human development out of animalism
there did exist the stronger instincts of the
brute, we might expect to find the traces to-

---

[1] The figures for Italy are inclusive of both legitimate
and illegitimate births.

day wherever passion is more powerful than
the respect due to custom, religion, and law.

TABLE IX.—ILLEGITIMATE BIRTHS. OF EACH 1,200 AN-
NUALLY, HOW MANY WERE DUE TO CONCEPTIONS AT
DIFFERENT SEASONS OF THE YEAR IN THE FOLLOW-
ING COUNTRIES?

	France.	Norway.	Sweden.	Holland.
SPRING—March, April, May	321	298	315	341
SUMMER—June, July, August	324	312	338	304
AUTUMN—Sept., Oct., Nov.	275	292	275	253
WINTER—Dec., Jan., Feb..	280	298	272	302
	1,200	1,200	1,200	1,200

The phenomenon is even more notable if we
compare the four months of April, May, June,
and July, when the proclivity appears strongest,
with the four months, October, November, December, and January, when it is least.

TABLE X.—OF EACH 1,200 BIRTHS ANNUALLY, HOW MANY
WERE THE RESULT OF CONCEPTIONS DURING TWO
PERIODS OF FOUR MONTHS EACH?

	Four months, April to July.		Four months, October to January.	
	Legitimate.	Illegitimate.	Legitimate.	Illegitimate.
France . .	429	446	384	365
Holland . .	436	437	384	364
Sweden . .	421	443	389	349
Norway [1] . .	425	419	397	396

For Italy we are unable to make, as regards
season, any distinction between legitimate and
illegitimate births, so that I have not included
it in the foregoing table. Taking all births
together, however, Italy tells the same story.
Per 1,200 annual births, the conceptions between April and July were 440, as contrasted
with 379 for the four months October to January.

In Norway, too, the spring-time is long in
coming, and its influence, as we should naturally

---

[1] For Norway the four months of strongest tendency for
illegitimate births are June to September. For the facts
from which the last three tables have been made, see Dr.
Bertillon's article "Natalité," in *Dict. Enc. des Sciences
Medicales.*

expect, is felt at a period considerably later than in other countries.

While there are no English statistics available which allow exact comparison with those mentioned for other nations, we are nevertheless given by the Registrar General the basis for what seems to me an exceedingly interesting curve diagram, in the quarterly birth-rate since 1841. Merely as figures they appear to have attracted no attention; but thrown into a diagram, the singular alternations from season to season are most strikingly evident. It appears that for the ten years 1841–50 the average birth-rate in England and Wales for the first quarter of the year was 34·2; that for the second quarter it was 33·7; at once falling away for the last half of the year to an average of 31·2. Now see how regularly this phenomenon is repeated for the next forty years, and then how closely it compares with the experience of half a century. For the quarterly birth-rate in England and Wales for over fifty years forms a succession of similar waves, from season to season.

Curve Diagram, showing for England and Wales the Annual Birth-Rate to 1,000 living, for each Quarter of the Year, during Four Ten-Year Periods.[1]

Birth Rate.	1841-'50				1851-'60				1861-'70				1871-'80.			
	1	2	3	4	1	2	3	4	1	2	3	4	1	2	3	4
37																
36									●				●			
35					●	●				●				●		
34	●										●				●	●
33		●										●				
32							●	●								
31			●	●												
30																

We have thus a diagram based upon nearly *thirty million births*. It proves, I think,

----

[1] The curve showing the birth-rate variations for more than half a century may be easily made by the reader on a sheet of ruled paper, from the following data. The average number of births during the first three months of the period 1838–1889 was at the annual rate of 351 per ten thousand population; for the next three months, April to June, 349; while for the third quarter the rate was only 327, and for the last quarter, 326. See Table 4, in Reg. Gen. Rep. for England and Wales for 1889. See also Table No. 15 in the 39th Annual Report of the Registrar General for year 1876.

beyond question the influence of the seasons upon the birth-rate in this country. Taken altogether, the facts seem to me almost definitely conclusive of the theory that as regards births, male or female, in city or country, legitimate or illegitimate, in countries as far apart as Italy and England or France and Sweden, the months of spring and summer mark on the human race a stronger propulsion toward what Schopenhauer calls "the will to live."

Marriage.—One would naturally expect to find the influence of season particularly noticeable upon the marriage rate. In a perfectly natural system of society, where the inclination or proclivity was free to turn undisturbed, it would be undoubtedly evident. It so happens, however, that religious and social customs intervene in most civilized countries, and create prejudices for, or against, the celebration of marriage during particular seasons of the year, —prejudices which of course have no basis in nature. For instance, in Catholic countries marriage must not take place during Lent; therefore in France and Italy the majority of nuptials are in February. In Ireland, particu-

larly in the West and South, more than half
the Catholic marriages are celebrated between
Christmas and Shrovetide.   In some parts of
Europe, Scotland for instance, there is a strong
prejudice against marrying in May—a prejudice
which Sir Walter Scott noticed in Malta, and
mentions in his last journals.   Nearly everywhere agricultural populations object to the
season of harvest, and defer such ceremonies
until October and November.   In Russia more
than three-fourths of all marriages occur in
autumn and winter; a proportion altogether
impossible unless some exceedingly strong local
customs or religious prejudices did not inter-
fere.   No such prejudice appears in respect
to criminal actions; it does not appear that
intending suicides hesitate because it happens
to be Lent.   There is no doubt, I think, that
an influence toward marriage is exerted by
different seasons—an influence which is per-
ceptible in several countries—but as a rule it
is quite overwhelmed and repressed, or rather
diverted, by considerations of policy, local prejudices, and the dictates of religion.

Upon the tendency to marital dissatisfaction,
one might expect the influence of spring-time

to be specially felt. Are elopements more common at this season? There are no figures, and of course no means of deciding the facts. In his valuable study of the divorce question, Dr. J. Bertillon has given the season of the years during which some 7,177 divorces were pronounced in France during the two years 1885–86. Of this number it appears that no less than 61 per cent. were obtained between April 1st and September 30th of each year, leaving for the autumn and winter 39 per cent. Do these figures indicate to any extent the period of the year when divorce proceedings were initiated? If so, they accord with the general law. Usually, however, so much delay intervenes between the application for divorce and its concession, that little relation may exist between the time when desire for disunion first shaped action, and the time of the year. Still the coincidence is worth noting, and makes further observation desirable.

In other phases of conduct springing from emotional excitement we perhaps may detect in some slight degree the working of the general law. Duels, for instance, would not at first glance be taken as subject to any law of periodicity. In Italy, nevertheless, it is found that they are far more common in spring and summer than in the other seasons, and particularly frequent in spring.

Popular insurrections, riots, outbursts of patriotic fervour, or revolutions, all are apparently more apt to occur in the spring and summer months. In America, it has been noticed that the first armed resistance to British authority was made in April, 1775, that the first pitched battle was fought in June, and that the decision to sever absolutely all allegiance to the mother country was adopted in July. It may some day be held doubtful whether that great wave of patriotic fury which swept over the Northern States at the firing upon Fort Sumter in April, 1861, could possibly have been evoked at the North during the chilly months of November and December. Four great riots in the city of New York, in 1849, 1857, 1863, and 1871, occurred during May, June, and July. In Paris, it was July that witnessed the attack upon the Bastille in 1789, the fall of the Bourbons in 1830, and that declaration of war with Prussia in 1870 which led to the overthrow of Napoleon III., while

the great riot of June, 1848, which overturned
the Orleans dynasty, and the final scenes of
the Commune in the closing days of May,
1871—tragedies and atrocities which it almost
seems as if civilization had conspired with
history to forget—all these are in conformity
with the influence of spring and summer on the
passion toward violence.   It will not do to
push this part of the theory to absolute conclusions without a careful tabulation of all great
historical insurrectionary movements and political outbreaks throughout the Northern Hemi-
sphere, and for this I have no present leisure.
But the instances given are certainly fairly
representative of popular insurrectionary movements ; and if England has been omitted, it is
only because riots are always unusual here.
The last occasion of a great mob in London
was the "No-Popery" riot of June, 1780.   Certainly, as a rule, so far as popular outbreaks are
concerned, winter seems to be conservative in
its influence, while spring and summer are full
of passionate tendencies toward outbreak,
whether of riot or revolution.

For a final comparison I have grouped
together various phases of conduct, wherein

TABLE XI.—OF EACH THOUSAND (1,000) ATTACKS OF
INSANITY OR CASE OF SUICIDE, CRIME, ETC., HOW
MANY HAPPENED IN EACH HALF OF THE YEAR?

Phases of Conduct or Disease.	Six Months of Spring and Summer.	Six Months of Autumn and Winter.	The Year.
INSANITY.			
(¹) Dr. Ritti's Admissions to Charenton, 10 yrs. (1879–88) . .	**52·6**	47·4	100·0
Esquirols	**54·8**	45 2	100·0
(¹) Pennsylvania Hospital admissions (7,867 cases)	**54·5**	45·5	100·0
(¹) Scotland. Admissions to Asylums, 10 yrs. (1865–74), men .	**52·7**	47 3	100·0
(¹) Scotland. Admissions to Asylums, 10 yrs. (1865–74), women.	**53·3**	46·7	100·0
(¹) Scotland. Admissions to Asylums, 8 yrs. (1880–87), men .	**52·9**	47·1	100·0
(¹) Scotland. Admissions to Asylums, 8 yrs. (1880–87), women.	**53·8**	46·2	100·0
SUICIDE.			
London. 20 years (1865–84) [Dr. Ogle]	**55·9**	44·1	100·0
(¹) New York, 10 years (1870–79) .	**55·3**	44·7	100·0
(¹) ,, ,, ,, ,, (1880–89) .	**54·9**	45·1	100·0
(¹) San Francisco, 10 years (1871–80)	**52·4**	47·6	100·0
France, 17 years (1836–52), men.	**58·8**	41·2	100·0
France, 17 years (1836–52), women	**57·9**	42·1	100·0
(¹) Switzerland, 10 years (1876–85).	**57·4**	42 6	100·0
(¹) Denmark ,, ,, ,, (April–Sept., 6 months) . . .	**59·5**	40·5	100·0
Belgium (1841–49).	**57·6**	42·4	100·0
(¹) Italy, 3 years (1880–82) . . .	**57·6**	42·4	100·0
(¹) Japan, 4 years (1882–85) [22,894 cases].	**57·4**	42·6	100·0

Phases of Conduct or Disease.	Six Months of Spring and Summer.	Six Months of Autumn and Winter.	The Year.
SUICIDE—*continued.*			
([1]) Japan, 3 years (1886–88) [18,204 cases]	58·6	41·4	100·0
Algiers, 4 years (1879–82) . .	61·0	39·0	100·0
([1]) England and Wales, *attempts* at suicide (1878–1887)	60·4	39·6	100·0
HOMICIDE (including murderous assaults).			
([1]) England and Wales, 5 years (1878–82)	54·1	45·9	100·0
([1]) England and Wales, 5 years (1883–87)	54·9	45·1	100·0
CRIME.			
([1]) England and Wales, crime agt. person, 5 years (1878–82) . .	54·0	46·0	100·0
([1]) England and Wales, crime agt. person, 5 years (1883–87) . .	54·9	45·1	100·0
([1]) Ireland, crime agt. person, 10 years (1878–87)	53·4	46·6	100·0
France, crime agt. person, 40 years (1830–69)	55·0	45·0	100·0
([1]) England and Wales, crimes agt. chastity, 10 years (1878–87) .	60·1	39·9	100·0
France, crimes agt. chastity, 10 years (1860–69)	62·9	37·1	100·0
BIRTHS.			
Illegitimate, France, 1856–65 .	53·7	46·3	100·0
„ Holland, 1860–69	53·7	46·3	100·0
„ Sweden, 1861–70 .	54·5	45·5	100·0
„ Paris, 1856–65 .	51·8	48·2	100·0
Legitimate and illegitimate, Italy	52·7	47·3	100·0
Legitimate and illegitimate, England and Wales (51 years)	51·9	48·1	100·0

[1] See footnote on page 128.

statistics covering long periods of time show what is the preponderance of occurrence during spring and summer as compared with the remainder of the year. It is manifest to any one, that if no influence of the kind was in existence, the normal frequency of each phase of conduct for each half of the year would be exactly half, or 500 in each thousand cases during the year. In the preceding table I have included some statistics to which no previous reference in detail has been made.[1]

This list might be indefinitely extended, but here at least is enough to demonstrate that some force or influence disturbs the even distribution throughout the year of certain phases of conduct, and especially of conduct arising from passions which, in excess, are probably allied to madness. This preponderance is not very great, but it is constant, year after year. Perhaps we might even measure the potency of that inclination toward violent actions exerted by the warmer seasons; for it is about the difference between the highest and lowest

---

[1] All statistics thus distinguished have been gathered by the author from the original official documents. In most cases the exact figures will be found in the Appendix.

averages. During ten years for example, the number of Crimes against the Person, in England and Wales, during the first quarter of the year were 6,471, or an average for the year of about 25,800. As a matter of fact the number was over 30,000. In Scotland again, during eighteen years the number of persons attacked with insanity during December was 2,971, and during January, 2,974. Now had the disease exhibited no greater rate of prevalence throughout the other months, *more than* 3,000 *patients* would have probably escaped the need for asylums in Scotland alone! But even immunity from insanity would be perhaps too dearly purchased at the cost of perpetual winters.

Are we justified in supposing that the influence of season is limited only to crime, insanity, etc.? If what we sometimes call the "unreasoning impulses" are pushed into undue activity as winter leaves us and the earth responds to solar influences, may not other actions, infinitely more numerous arise from the same cause? To one deed of crime, so serious as to call for the notice of the law, there are ten thousand acts of impetuous folly, of

K

unreasoning anger, of jealousy, bad temper, and pugnacious proclivity. There can be no statistical record of them; yet they may ruin the happiness of a million homes. We can only appeal to individual experience. If attention were generally directed to the inquiry, we might find here, as well as elsewhere, that proclivity towards all passionate or emotional acts is strongest at certain seasons, in conformity with that general law, which then increases the frequency of insanity, vice, and crime.

What is the underlying cause of the phenomena I have grouped together? Admitting the facts, why does the cycle of the seasons thus affect the human will? How is it that at one time impulse is chilled with cold, and at another season heated into fierce activity?

The connection between the periodicity of attacks of insanity and proclivity toward suicide has more than once been suggested. If suicide be invariably the result of insane impulse, we can easily comprehend why the act of despair follows the course of the mental disease. As previously pointed out, attempts made to separate suicides of persons manifestly insane from others, have only resulted in discovering that both classes of self-destruction are alike subject to this annual ebb and flow.

I am nevertheless inclined to believe in the close relationship between the great mass of criminal, vicious, and passionate acts, arising from the violence of the emotions, and an unsound mental condition. It need not be that complex and completely abnormal state which we call "insanity." One of the principal lecturers on mental diseases in London, was accustomed to advise his pupils to avoid pronouncing upon the insanity of any one; it was far safer, he declared, to affirm that the patient affected was of "unsound mind," a term of great flexibility, and of corresponding utility. It may not be too much to assume that all violent and sudden outbursts of unreasoning rage, cruelty, lust, or jealousy, leading to actions which the perpetrator in sober moments bitterly regrets, are the effect of a mind *temporarily unbalanced, and unsound.* A mad man is a madman for the hour; he does not reason or reflect : he only feels ; and even the certainty of retributive justice may not check the uplifted hand. The mentally unbalanced who sooner or later find themselves within the walls of an asylum or retreat are but a tithe of those who escape such control, and continue year after year to make miserable the lives of all dependent upon them. But even granting this connection between "insanity" and acts of passion, we have still to ascertain why such attacks of mental unsoundness vary with the seasons ? What mysterious bond unites them all in one common perturbation at certain seasons of the year ?

There is one hypothesis which seems to me capable of accounting for all the phenomena. It is this ; that either by the gradual increase of solar light and solar heat, or else in some other manner quite mysterious at present, the breaking up of winter and the advent of spring and summer seasons, produces upon all animated nature a peculiar state of excitement or exaltation of the nervous system. Upon evidence not yet sufficient for demonstration, I am disposed to believe that one effect both in higher animals and in man is an actual increase in the quantity of blood sent through the system ; or that the heart in reality beats at a quicker rate, with stronger impulse, in April and May, than in November and December.

Now the physiological effect of this slightly increased nervous energy and sensibility manifests itself probably in different ways. In the first place everywhere in nature the advent of the warmer seasons signalizes the special aptitude of the creature for fertility and reproduction ; and the facts I have brought forward appear to me to indicate that mankind does not escape an influence which thus affects alike the animal and vegetable world. Doubtless in many cases the influence is too slight to be subjectively noted ; we can only discover the effect through statistics of conduct, in relation to the great mass of human beings, and by noting whether there is in truth any preponderance of phenomena at different seasons.

Again, a continuous and gradually increasing wave of excitability or nervous exaltation affecting the entire human race in any given latitude would undoubtedly give rise to emotional manifestations, leading to action. Probably there are few of us who have not at certain times experienced a strange tendency to melancholy retrospect, a vague restlessness, an undue depression of spirits, or an irritability and discontent without apparent cause. Whether conduct thus incited shall be good or bad, generous or selfish, vicious or virtuous, will in all cases principally depend on individual character and organization.   To humanity in the highest type of development, perhaps even to the Race as a whole, this exacerbation of emotional life with the opening year does no harm ; on the contrary, it is the source of sentiment, the occasion of poetry, the inspiration in gentle natures of the purest and most reverential love, or in noble souls of patriotic resistance to oppression and tyranny.   But that which upon the great mass of mankind evinces itself in perfectly normal ways, may have a far different effect upon the ungovernable temper, the uncontrolled appetite, the jealous suspicions of unsound minds.   Discontent with environment becomes then transformed, it may be, into desire for death, and the thought of suicide.   Disappointed love may then lead to a fixed melancholy, or anxiety and trouble to the delusion of despair, and we then say that a wave of insanity passed over us.   The brutal lusts, the selfish and pugnacious instincts of the half-civilized barbarians in our great cities, may need only the incitement of opportunity to induce the trampling under foot of all moral restraints; and we note the increase of crimes of lust and resentment, or of murders and assaults with intent to kill. Like the magnetic needle, the will trembles toward every impulse; and when brutal propensities are uncontrolled, even slight causes may be sufficient to decide the sway and determine the action. For it depends where one stands whether he shall feel even the strongest of impulses in the physical world. The earthquake that laid Lisbon in ruins was noticed by the peasants working in their vineyards a hundred miles away only as a slight, tremulous thrill.

The hypothetical connection between certain phases of conduct may, perhaps, be brought more distinctly before the mind of the reader by the scheme on the following page.

Misapprehension in regard to any unfamiliar theory is almost certain to occur. It took many years for popular comprehension to understand that the Darwinian hypothesis did not mean the lineal and direct descent of men from monkeys. It cannot therefore be too clearly stated that cosmic influence upon human conduct *is always very slight when we take into*

Theory of Relation between Solar Influences and Human Conduct.

I. Solar Influences.	II. Physical results upon Men and Animals.	III. Mental and Physical conditions arising from II.	IV. Slight preponderance of certain phases of conduct or disease in *Spring* and *Summer* produced thereby.
Gradually increasing LIGHT and HEAT OF SPRING AND SUMMER.	I. INCREASED ACTION OF THE HEART. II. EXCITATION OF THE NERVOUS SYSTEM.	1. Emotional exaltation. 2. Increased tendency toward the reproductive instinct. 3. Increased tendency toward JEALOUSY. 4. Increased combativeness and pugnacity. 5. Increased irritability of disposition and temper 6. Sentimentality. 7. Mental depression. 8. Enthusiasm for change.	1. Birth-rate, legitimate. 2. Birth-rate, illegitimate. 3. Crimes of sex-passion. 4. *Marriage rate?* 5. Divorces. 6. Murders. 7. Assaults. 8. Duels. 9. Riots. 10. Attacks of insanity. 11. "*Love affairs?*" 12. Suicide. 13. Attempts at suicide. 14. Revolutions.

account the totality of action in any direction. What appears to me clear is its existence as a true factor of causation—no matter to how slight an extent. Only by some theory of the kind do I see how we are to explain phenomena of life—such for instance as the birth-rate, and suicide—which have no conceivable relation to each other, and yet which alike preponderate at certain seasons of the year.

But even if true, what is the use of knowing it ?   No greater use, perhaps, than in other interrogations of Nature ;   in the study of the habits of an earth-worm, the flight of a swallow, or the parallax of a star.   Yet I fancy there is always a potential value in facts.

Of their relation to life, animals must always remain in ignorance ; but to human beings the knowledge which future investigation of these questions may more   completely attain—that they are   periodically   subject   to   influences, dangerous oftentimes in their final effect upon conduct—cannot be wholly valueless.   And besides this, there seems to me something so profoundly wonderful in the secrets of Nature and the uniformity of natural laws, that I envy no one whose emotions are never touched by that   sense   of   mystery   which   underlies   all reverence and love.   One summer's day the opportunity was mine to look through a tele-scope at a large spot on the sun.   Into that dark chasm our planet might drop, without even touching the edge of flame on either side. That may yet be its fate.   But even now, it is not impossible that what we call "a mere sun-spot" in midsummer may have some influence, in our little world, upon the ebb and flow of passion, the excitement of emotion, and all that makes up the profound mystery of human life.

APPENDIX I.

EXTRACTS.

Illegitimacy in England.

No one can have taken any interest in the working-classes without being aware how frightfully common among them is what they term "a misfortune;" how few young women come to the marriage altar at all, or come there just a week or two before maternity, or having already had several children, often only half-brothers and sisters. * * * It is easy for tenderly reared young ladies who study human passions through Miss Austen or Miss Edgeworth to say, " How shocking! Oh, it can't be true!" But it *is* true, and they will not live many more years without finding it true.

Another fact, stranger still to account for, is, that *the women who thus fall are by no means the worst of their station.* I have heard it affirmed by more than one lady, and by one in particular whose experience is as large as her benevolence, that many of them are of the very best— refined, intelligent, truthful, and affectionate.

" I don't know how it is," she would say, " whether their very superiority makes them dissatisfied with their own rank, so that they fall easier victims to the rank above them, or whether other virtues can exist and flourish entirely distinct from, and after the loss of what we are accustomed to believe the indispensable virtue of our sex,—Chastity. I cannot explain it; I can only say that it is so—that some of my most promising village girls have been the first to come to harm; and some of the best and most faithful servants I ever had have been girls who have fallen into shame, and who, had I not gone to the rescue, and put them on the way to do well, would invariably have become *lost women.*"

Had she not "come to the rescue." Rescue, then, is possible, and they were capable of being rescued. ["A Woman's Thoughts about Women," by Miss Mulock, Author of "John Halifax, Gentleman."]

Immorality (in Hayti) is so universal that it almost ceases to be a fault, for a fault implies an exception, and in Hayti it is the rule. Young people make experiment of one another before they will enter into any closer connexion. *So far they are no worse than in our own English Islands, where the custom is equally general.* [Froude's "History of English in West Indies," p. 344.]

ILLEGITIMACY IN SCOTLAND.

In Scotland, incontinency subjects the offending parties to ecclesiastical measures. The ministers and elders of a parish call before them the mothers and the putative fathers (when discovered) of all illegitimate children, admonish them seriously for their conduct, and *exclude them from participation in the ordinance of bread and wine* until they have expressed contrition for their offence. [Rep. of Poor Law Commissioners to Sir G. Grahame, 1844.]

In a paper read by Dr. Stark, upon the Vital Statistics of Scotland, the writer gave the result of an inquiry into Illegitimacy in certain parishes of that country. "In seventy-nine parishes there were *among the members of the Established Church* 4,305 births, and of these 328 were illegitimate!" ["Journal of the Statistical Society," Vol. 14.]

NOTE.—That is a rate of 78 per 1000, higher than that of France or Italy.

Peasant Morality in Denmark.

With regard to the peasant population of the rural districts
. . . it was found that of a hundred first-born children no
less than thirty-nine were born under seven months after
marriage, to which must be added nine (9) per cent. born
between seven and nine months after marriage.   A great
number of the brides who were not pregnant at marriage
had already had illegitimate children with the bridegroom
or others ; so that it may probably be assumed that *in two-
thirds of the marriages* (childless marriages excepted) *the
bride had had children while unmarried, or was pregnant at
the marriage.*   ["Westergaard on Marriage Statistics of Denmark,"
Copenhagen.   Translation furnished to Seventh International Congress of Hygiene and Demography.]

Child Murder.

An inquest was held before Mr. Braxton Hicks, at the
Star and Garter, Battersea, concerning the death of a female
child whose body was found in the Thames.   Dr. Kempster
stated that he saw the body at the mortuary, and had made
a *post mortem* examination.   The bones of the skull had
been fractured all over, and the nose was flattened on the
face.   The injuries were inflicted *while the child was alive,*
and they were the cause of death.   The Coroner: "I think
we have had about ten similar cases, have we not?"   Dr.
Kempster: "Yes; *all killed in the same way.*"   The
Coroner : "In these cases as soon as a child is born its
head is knocked all to pieces, and the body then thrown
into the river."   The jury returned a verdict of "Wilful
murder against some person or persons unknown." [*London
Times,* February 5, 1891.]

Distressing Suicide.—A well-dressed young woman
was found lying on a seat at Rugby Station, Tuesday night.

She had evidently taken some carbolic acid from a bottle which was by her side. Death ensued in half an hour. A number of letters were found in her possession, some signed " Your loving husband, Jack ——."

Dr. Wynter held an inquest on the body of the young woman who committed suicide at Rugby Station. A young man named Allen, employed as a cook at Oxford, stated that last summer the deceased and himself were living at Douglas, Isle of Man. In September they left Douglas, and *for over a fortnight they lived together as husband and wife at the deceased's parents', the girl's relatives thinking they were married.* Dr. Simpson expressed the opinion that the deceased was *enceinte.* The jury returned a verdict of " Suicide while temporarily insane." The Coroner, address-ing Allen, said that though he was not legally responsible for her death, he was morally responsible. He lived with her in a barefaced manner as her husband, and then de-serted her, and in her distracted condition she took her life. [*Oxford Chronicle*, January 31st, 1891.]

NOTE.—In the State of New York, by thus living "with her in a barefaced manner as her husband," and acknowledging that relation to her parents, this man would have become her legal husband without further ceremony.

CRUEL TREATMENT OF A CHILD.—At the Denbighshire Assizes yesterday, before Justice Lawrence, Catherine Roberts, aged 30 years, a charwoman, of Abergele, was charged with murdering her *illegitimate* female child, aged seven years. The medical evidence went to show that the child had been subjected to a long treatment of ill-usage, there being no less than 86 bruises on her body. Wit-nesses were called, and deposed to seeing the accused throw the deceased over a stile, whilst on another occasion it was alleged she beat the girl with a stick. When examined, there was not the slightest trace of food in the stomach of the deceased.—The jury found the prisoner "Guilty of manslaughter," and she was sentenced to twenty years' imprisonment. [*Daily News*, July 23rd, 1891.]

At Stratford Petty Sessions, Annie Smith, 21, a respectably-dressed person, described as a servant of Quarry Cottage, Coursley Wood, Wadhurst, Sussex, was charged with attempting to drown her child, Charles Smith, aged one month, by throwing it into a ditch on Wanstead Flats. Joseph Wood, of 28, Francis Street, Stratford, the manager of a working-men's home, said that at about a quarter to 6 o'clock on Thursday evening he was going towards Forest-gate across Wanstead Flats, when he saw the prisoner coming along the road. She had a baby in her arms. She passed him, and when he had gone a little way, he turned round and looked back. He then saw the prisoner go down a bank. She still had the baby in her arms. She took a cloak off the baby and put it (the cloak) on the grass, and then she disappeared from his sight. Soon afterwards she came up the bank again and went across the road. Then she ran towards Epping Forest. He ran after her, and when he got up to her, he asked her what she had done with the child. She said, "I have thrown it into the ditch." He said, "You had better come back with me while I get the child out," and she walked back with him until they came to the spot where she had disappeared. He then saw the child, and at once went across the ditch and got it out of the water. He thought there were between three and four feet of water in the ditch. The child was lying in the water, floating, with its hands up. He got hold of one of its hands to pull it out. Then he patted it on the back to get the water out of it. Giving it

to the prisoner, he took her to the Leyton Police-station, and there she was charged. Prisoner was remanded.
[*The Times*, February 14th, 1891.]

Yesterday, at Northampton, before Mr. Justice Vaughan Williams, Emily Scott, aged 20, *a domestic servant*, was charged with the murder of her infant child. Mr. Sills and Mr. Perceval Keep, instructed by the Solicitor to the Treasury, appeared for the prosecution ; and the prisoner was defended by Mr. Toller. It appeared that on the 8th of June last the prisoner, who had for two years been in the service of Mrs. Bird, at Welford, had done a hard day's work, but in the evening she complained of feeling ill, and went to bed early. Shortly afterwards her mistress went up to her room and found her very ill. A doctor was sent for, and he discovered in a cupboard the body of a fully grown female child, which had been newly born. The body was wrapped in an apron, the strings of which were drawn *round the neck of the child*, and a handkerchief was *stuffed into its mouth*. It was placed just inside the cupboard, which was closed, but not locked. The medical evidence showed that, although in the opinion of the doctor the death of the child had been caused by the handkerchief and apron strings, it was *impossible for him to say whether it had had a separate existence or not.* Upon this evidence the charge of murder was abandoned by the prosecution, and the case was left to the jury on the question of conceal-ment of birth. The jury found the prisoner *Not Guilty*, and she was discharged ! [*The Times*, July 2nd, 1891.]

ANCESTRY OF PRESIDENT LINCOLN.

On the subject of his ancestry and origin I only remem-ber one time when Mr. Lincoln ever referred to it. It was about 1850, when he and I were driving in his one-horse buggy to the court in Menard county, Illinois. The suit we were going to try was one in which we were likely, either directly or collaterally, to touch upon the subject of hereditary traits. During the ride he spoke, for the first time in my hearing, of his mother, dwelling on her characteristics, and mentioning or enumerating what qualities he inherited from her. He said, among other things, that *she was the illegitimate daughter of Lucy Hanks* and a well-bred Virginia farmer or planter ; and he argued that from this last source came his power of analysis, his logic, his mental activity, his ambition, and all the qualities that distinguished him from the other members and descendants of the Hanks family. His theory in discussing the matter of hereditary traits had been that, for certain reasons, illegitimate children are oftentimes sturdier and brighter than those born in lawful wedlock ; and in his case, he believed that his better nature and finer qualities came from this broad-minded, unknown Virginian.

During and after the Presidential campaign of 1860, Lincoln repeatedly refused to furnish any details regarding his progenitors. [" Herndon's Life of Abraham Lincoln."]

APPENDIX II.

On the Value of Statistics.

" It is hardly possible to overrate the value of figures, partly by checking that universal tendency to exaggeration —not wilful, but a kind of mental illusion—which operates wherever we are deeply interested; partly as giving definiteness and precision to ideas which otherwise would remain floating in our minds in a vague, and therefore comparatively useless, form.

" When you find uniformity, or something which closely approximates to uniformity, it is impossible not to be impressed with the permanence and steadiness of the laws which regulate our existence." [Lord Derby, before the British Association.]

Illegitimacy in Europe.

Of each 1000 Births (still-births excluded) during years mentioned, how many were illegitimate in the following countries?

	1869.	1870.	1885.	1886.	1887.	1888.	1889.
Ireland	29	27	28	27	28	29	28
Russia	28	28	28	27	28	27	27
Holland	36	35	31	32	32	31	33
Switzerland *	—	—	50	49	48	48	47
England and Wales .	58	56	48	47	48	46	46
Spain	56	55	—	—	—	—	—
Italy	60	64	76	75	75	74	73
France	75	75	80	82	82	85	84
Belgium	71	72	87	87	88	87	88
Prussia *	78	79	82	82	82	80	80
Hungary	70	68	84	83	84	84	85
Scotland	98	96	85	82	83	81	79
Norway.	85	91	79	79	77	76	74
Denmark	114	111	100	97	97	93	93
Sweden	102	104	104	102	105	102	101
Saxony.	136	137	130	129	128	125	125
Bavaria *	179	164	139	139	138	140	141
Austria.	138	131	147	147	147	146	147

* Including Still Births for 1885–89.

Note.—In the above table are grouped together the latest available statistics for the principal countries of Europe. For purposes of comparison the illegitimate birth-rate of twenty years ago is also given, and the reader will thus be able to see the differences between the races of Europe, and to note to what extent the present tendency of each nationality is toward increase or decrease of its illegitimate births.

AVERAGE ANNUAL ILLEGITIMATE BIRTHS DURING TEN YEARS [1869–1878] TO 1000 UNMARRIED WOMEN IN EACH COUNTY, AGED 15–45. AVERAGE FOR ENGLAND AND WALES, **15·8**.

[From Registrar-General's Report for 1881.]

Counties with Illegitimate Rates below the Average of England.		Counties with Illegitimate Rates above the Average, but below 20·0.		Counties with Illegitimate Rates above 20·0.	
Surrey (extra-metrop.)	8·9	Cheshire	16·1	Suffolk	20·2
Middlesex (extra-metrop.)	8·9	Rutlandshire	16·2	North Wales	20·5
LONDON	10·1	Hertfordshire	16·7	Northumberland	20·5
Gloucestershire	12·1	Buckinghamshire	17·0	Westmoreland	20·6
Somersetshire	12·1	Monmouthshire	17·2	Lincolnshire	20·7
Sussex	12·3	South Wales	17·3	East Riding (York)	20·9
Devonshire	12·9	Huntingdonshire	17·4	Derbyshire	21·2
Hampshire	13·0	Northamptonshire	17·8	Durham	21·6
Kent (extra-metrop.)	13·7	Oxfordshire	18·0	Staffordshire	22·6
Dorsetshire	13·7	Cambridgeshire	18·3	Nottinghamshire	23·1
Warwickshire	14·4	Leicestershire	18·6	Norfolk	25·0
Essex	14·8	West Riding (York)	18·6	Shropshire	25·8
Cornwall	15·2	Bedfordshire	19·0	North Riding (York)	26·4
Lancashire	15·3	Herefordshire	19·3	Cumberland	27·2
Berkshire	15·4				
Worcestershire	15·5				
Wiltshire	15·6				

NOTE.—"The examination of this Table reveals a curious fact in regard to the geographical distribution of Illegitimacy. If an outline map of England and Wales be taken, in which the county boundaries are distinguished, it will be found that a continuous, though irregular, line can be drawn from the east coast between Essex and Suffolk, across England to the British Channel; and that while *every county below this line, without exception, has an illegitimate rate below the average, every county above it, with only one exception* (viz., Lancashire), *has a rate above the average.*"

ILLEGITIMACY, ENGLAND AND WALES.

Of each 1000 Births during 10 years, 1879–1888, in each county, how many were Illegitimate?

(See Map facing Title-page.)

Counties having a rate *less* than 48 (average for England and Wales).		Counties having an Illegitimate Birth-rate—					
		Between 48-57.		Between 58-67.		Over 68.	
Essex .	34	Derby .	48	Lincoln .	58	North Wales .	69
Middlesex (extra-metrop.) .	35	Leicester .	48	East Riding (York) .	58	Westmoreland .	70
Surrey .	40	Dorset .	49	Nottingham .	59	Norfolk .	74
Warwick .	41	Wilts .	49	North Riding (York) .	60	Cumberland .	76
Durham .	41	Stafford .	49	Cornwall .	62	Hereford .	76
Monmouth .	42	Huntingdon .	49	Bedford .	67	Shropshire .	82
Kent (extra-metrop.) .	43	Berkshire .	49				
Somerset .	43	Worcester .	50				
Hants .	43	Rutland .	51				
Lancaster .	45	West Riding (York) .	51				
Gloucester .	45	Bucks .	51				
South Wales .	45	Sussex .	52				
Northampton .	46	Cheshire .	52				
Devon .	47	Hertford .	53				
		Northumberland .	54				
		Oxford .	54				
		Cambridge .	54				
		Suffolk .	57				

Compiled from Table No. 10, Registrar-General's Report, No. LII.

ILLEGITIMATE BIRTHS IN CITIES OF ENGLAND.

Years.	London.			Birmingham.			Liverpool.		
	Total Births.	Illegitimate.	Ratio to 1000.	Total Births.	Illegitimate.	Ratio to 1000 Total Births.	Total Births.	Illegitimate.	Ratio to 1000 Total Births.
1879	131,542	5,115	39	9,514	377	39	7,555	343	45
1880	133,310	5,173	39	9,240	396	42	7,307	346	47
1881	132,904	5,188	39	9,081	405	45	6,944	355	51
1882	133,309	5,217	39	9,049	397	44	6,696	341	51
1883	134,503	5,271	39	8,854	392	44	6,292	331	52
1884	135,651	5,137	38	8,911	368	41	6,499	377	58
1885	132,952	5,314	40	8,459	343	40	6,054	368	61
1886	134,339	5,116	38	8,644	379	43	6,023	368	61
1887	133,359	5,307	40	8,198	408	50	5,588	371	66
1888	131,761	4,964	38	7,639	404	53	5,456	313	57
1889	132,233	5,032	38	8,089	364	45	5,269	305	₿8
1890									
1891									
1892									

ILLEGITIMACY IN LONDON.

Of each thousand births in the following districts and sub-districts, how many were illegitimate ?

	1875.	1883.	1884.	1885.	1886.	1887.	1888.	1889.	1890.
Whitechapel . .	28	34	35	31	34	26	29	30	27
Marylebone . . .	115	146	166	180	168	178	158	172	168
Sub- { Rectory .	216	213	239	287	220	240	197	275	247
districts { St. Mary.	276	370	399	414	410	413	382	394	406
ALL LONDON . .	38	39	38	40	38	40	38	38	38

NOTE.—It will be seen from this table that in one part of London (St. Mary, Marylebone) the rate of illegitimacy is annually *over one-third of all the births*. The contrast between Whitechapel and Marylebone is noteworthy.

ILLEGITIMACY IN COUNTIES OF SCOTLAND.

Of each 1000 Births in each County, during period named, how many were illegitimate?

[Arranged in order of Illegitimate Birth-rate, 10 years, 1876–1885.]

Counties having a High Proportion of Illegitimacy, *i.e.*, over 10 per cent.

County.	1855.	10 yrs. 1876–1885.	1886.	1887.
Banff . . .	136	164	162	168
Wigtown. . .	123	159	165	182
Elgin. . .	104	153	149	152
Dumfries . .	135	147	138	139
Kirkcudbright	120	146	150	157
Aberdeen . .	131	137	142	132
Kincardine. .	129	125	123	124
Caithness . .	70	108	121	115
Roxburgh . .	95	108	94	112
Nairn . . .	112	106	146	94
Berwick . .	89	103	116	111
Kinross . .	168	102	103	40
Forfar . . .	89	100	99	80

Counties having a Medium Proportion of Illegitimacy, *i.e.*, above 7 and under 10 per cent.

County.	1855.	10 yrs. 1876–1885.	1886.	1887.
Clackmannan	72	75	72	61
Argyll . .	58	75	77	79
Ayr . . .	70	76	78	78
Linlithgow	76	76	77	68
Edinburgh .	70	76	74	79
Haddington .	81	77	71	77
Inverness .	56	79	72	89
Selkirk . .	57	81	69	88
Peebles . .	97	82	87	88
Perth . . .	92	94	95	94

Counties having a Low Proportion of Illegitimacy, *i.e.*, under 7 per cent.

County.	1855.	10 yrs. 1876–1885.	1886.	1887.
Ross & Cromarty	37	47	48	50
Shetland Isles .	32	52	53	48
Dumbarton . .	71	54	52	50
Renfrew . .	61	59	54	55
Orkney Isles. .	41	63	59	77
Bute . . .	67	66	65	68
Stirling . .	68	66	67	66
Sutherland .	25	68	48	76
Fife . . .	66	68	64	64
Lanark . . .	65	69	65	68

Compiled from Detailed Annual Reports of the Registrar-General for Scotland.

N.B.—The figures for 1887 in this table are correct: those given in Table IV. (page 16) are only approximate.

ILLEGITIMACY IN PRINCIPAL CITIES OF SCOTLAND.
[From Registrar General's Reports.]
Number of Illegitimate Births in proportion :

	To 1000 Total Births.				To 1000 Unmarried Women between 15-45.			
	Aber-deen.	Dundee.	Edin-burgh.	Glas-gow.	Aber-deen.	Dundee.	Edin-burgh.	Glas-gow.
1873–1882 (10 yrs.)	112	107	82	82	—	—	—	—
1883	98	108	88	81	23	21	15	24
1884	103	100	79	79	24	21	14	24
1885	109	110	90	82	26	21	16	24
1886	114	101	83	78	28	19	14	23
1887	106	104	85	83	24	18	15	23

ILLEGITIMACY AND AGE OF MOTHERS.

Of total illegitimate births in England and Wales during the year 1902, how many were the first-born children of mothers at each age, and of either social condition ?

Age-periods of Mothers.	Single Women.		Widows and Divorced.		Total Births at each Age Period.
	First Child.	Other than First Child.	First Child (Illegitimate).	Other than First Child (Illegitimate).	
15–19 . .					
20–24 . .					
25–29 . .					
30–34 . .					
35–50 . .					
Total . .					

NOTE.—This is merely a suggestion for a statistical table which should indicate the relation between illegitimate births and the ages of the mothers. No facts of this kind are at present anywhere to be obtained.

ILLEGITIMACY IN CERTAIN COUNTIES OF IRELAND, DURING TEN YEARS, 1879–1888.

[Compiled from Reports of the Registrar-General.]

County.	Total No. all Births (1879–1888). Ten Years.	Total Unmarried Females (15–45) at Census of 1881.	No. of Illegitimate Births (Ten Years.)	Rate of Illegitimacy.	
				To 1000 Total Births.	To each 10,000 Unmarried Women (15–45).
Mayo, Connaught	57,141	29,069	322	5	11·7
Sligo, ,,	20,249	11,649	163	8	14
Galway, ,,	53,215	27,655	556	10	20
Donegal, Ulster	42,887	28,503	670	16	23·5
Tyrone, ,,	40,170	32,002	1,666	41	52
Londonderry, ,,	39,164	27,259	1,790	46	66
Down, ,,	60,346	34,330	3,084	51	90
Antrim, ,,	122,585	69,593	6,583	52	94·6
Kerry, Munster	48,624	21,721	691	14	32
Clare ,,	29,749	15,851	443	15	28
Limerick ,,	42,300	25,501	1,148	27	45
ALL IRELAND	1,200,782	731,767	31,856	26·5	43·5

ENGLAND WALES.   CORONERS' INQUESTS ON INFANTS 1 YEAR
OLD AND UNDER.

	Legitimate.			Illegitimate.		
	Boys.	Girls.	Both.	Boys.	Girls.	Both.
1881	2,171	1,887	4,058	545	481	1,026
1882	2,222	1,943	4,165	482	428	910
1883	2,354	2,029	4,383	498	449	947
1884	2,359	1,969	4,328	560	481	1,041
1885	2,323	1,962	4,285	583	438	1,021
1886	2,482	2,009	4,491	541	534	1,075
1887	2,561	2,224	4,785	555	488	1,043
Total Inquests 7 years	16,472	14,023	30,495	3,764	3,299	7,063
No. of Inquests to each 1000 born of either class			5			24

SEASONS AND CONDUCT.

Of each thousand cases of SUICIDE in the following countries for periods named, what proportion occurred in each month?

(Months above the average have the percentage in bold-faced type.)

Month.	London[1] (20 years), 1865–1884.	New York[2] (20 years), 1871–1890.	Prussia,[3] 1869–1877.	Saxony,[3] 1877–1880.	France,[4] 1836–1852.	France,[5] 1856–1867.	France,[6] 1872–1878.	Italy,[7] 1877–1879.	Italy,[7] 1880–1882.
January . .	73	74	66	62	72	72	76	65	64
February .	71	65	62	63	67	75	66	76	79
March . .	**84**	80	**83**	80	**84**	**85**	**85**	79	**92**
April . .	**93**	**96**	**93**	**96**	**95**	**93**	**97**	**103**	**109**
May . .	**100**	**105**	**99**	**105**	**105**	**98**	**103**	**117**	**110**
June . .	**102**	89	**105**	**107**	**108**	**112**	**110**	**117**	**108**
July . .	**91**	**99**	**104**	**103**	**107**	**99**	**105**	**107**	**106**
August .	89	79	**92**	**102**	89	**85**	**86**	**85**	79
September .	77	81	82	89	75	77	74	70	64
October . .	77	75	81	73	73	75	74	64	67
November .	73	81	70	64	63	66	65	64	65
December .	70	76	63	56	62	63	59	52	57
The Year .	1,000	1,000	1,000	1,000	1,000	1,000	1,000	1,000	1,000

[1] Dr. Wm. Ogle, "Suicide in England and Wales," p. 17.
[2] Board of Health Report, 1891, p. 191.
[3] Von Oettinger's "Moralstatistik," p. 748.
[4] Doctor Lisle's "Du Suicide."
[5] Von Oettinger's "Moralstatistik," p. 748.
[6] Dict. Enc. des Sciences Medicales, Art. "Suicide."
[7] Statistica delle Cause di Morte. (Annual Reports.)

SEASONS AND CONDUCT.
SUICIDE IN ALGERIA AND JAPAN.

Seasons.	Suicides in Algeria, 1879–1882.[1]		Suicides in Japan, 1882–1888.[2]	
	Number.	Per Cent.	Number.	Per Cent.
March, April, May	151	30·5	11,677	28·4
June, July, August	151	30·5	12,188	29·6
September, October, November .	92	19·	9,070	22
December, January, February .	101	20·	8,253	20
Total	495	100·0	41,188	100·0

[1] See Kocher's "La Criminalité chez les Arabes."
[2] See "Résumé Statistique de l'Empire du Japon," for 1891.

SEASONS AND CONDUCT.
NUMBER OF ATTEMPTS AT SUICIDE IN ENGLAND AND WALES, 1878–1887.
[Compiled from Judicial Reports.]

Year.	January to March.	April to June.	July to September.	October to December.	Total.
1878	181	272	307	191	951
1879	202	268	334	196	1,000
1880	181	281	308	219	989
1881	167	283	332	202	984
1882	220	315	330	262	1,127
1883	217	323	296	232	1,068
1884	247	327	387	207	1,168
1885	232	332	366	220	1,150
1886	188	318	357	220	1,083
1887	234	375	375	229	1,213
Ten Years .	2,069	3,094	3,392	2,178	10,733
Percentage .	19·3	28·8	31·6	20·3	100·0

SEASONS AND LUNACY.

Number of Lunatics admitted into Asylums of Scotland for Ten Years (1865–74), and Eight Years (1880–87).[1]

	Ten Years, 1865-1874.		Eight Years, 1880-1887.		Eighteen Years' Total.	Per Cent. each Month.
	Males.	Females.	Males.	Females.		
January	679	654	814	827	2,974	7·7
February	673	779	770	817	3,039	7·9
March	689	817	796	912	3,214	8·3
April.	786	848	805	935	3,374	8·7
May	757	894	912	1,058	3,621	9·4
June	777	904	906	1,012	3,599	9·3
July	827	868	860	977	3,532	9·1
August	686	836	796	907	3,225	8·3
September	739	804	714	877	3,134	8·1
October	665	782	726	818	2,991	7·7
November	646	741	763	854	3,004	7·8
December	664	775	744	788	2,971	7·7
Total	8,588	9,702	9,606	10,782	38,678	100·0

[1] Reports of Board of Commissioners in Lunacy, SCOTLAND. 17th Report, p. 26, and 31st Report, p. 28.

SEASONS AND CONDUCT.

NUMBER OF MURDERS (of persons over one year), ATTEMPTS AT MURDER and CASES OF MANSLAUGHTER, England and Wales, during each quarter of the year.

[Compiled from Judicial Reports.]

Year.	January to March.	April to June.	July to September.	October to December.	Total.
1878	92	101	114	100	407
1879	71	93	107	95	366
1880	84	92	114	104	394
1881	73	98	121	90	382
1882	92	107	110	99	408
1883	76	102	95	93	366
1884	106	84	122	91	403
1885	91	109	117	106	423
1886	88	107	129	79	403
1887	90	102	104	100	396
Ten Years.	863	995	1,133	957	3,948

SEASONS AND CONDUCT.

ALL CRIMES AGAINST PERSONS (not involving Crimes against property), England and Wales.

[Compiled from Judicial Reports.]

Year.	January to March.	April to June.	July to September.	October to December.	Total.
1878	656	782	781	633	2,852
1879	528	675	743	719	2,665
1880	641	736	759	733	2,869
1881	582	722	842	732	2,878
1882	717	870	918	695	3,200
1883	617	704	793	705	2,819
1884	682	839	939	742	3,192
1885	630	755	956	848	3,189
1886	712	976	1090	881	3,659
1887	706	894	989	812	3,401
Ten Years.	6,471	7,953	8,810	7,490	30,724

SEASONS AND CONDUCT.

NUMBER OF CRIMES AGAINST CHASTITY (Assaults, Rape, etc.),
England and Wales, 1878–1887.

[Compiled from Table V. Judicial Reports.]

Year.	January to March.	April to June.	July to September.	October to December.	Total.
1878	127	168	167	105	567
1879	99	143	174	126	542
1880	140	181	182	123	626
1881	106	168	210	144	628
1882	139	206	254	101	700
1883	141	179	212	133	665
1884	143	248	256	156	803
1885	133	219	267	234	853
1886	234	368	442	271	1,315
1887	215	345	379	259	1,198
Ten Years.	1,477	2,225	2,543	1,652	7,897

CRIMES AGAINST CHASTITY (Assaults, etc.) in France.

Arranged by Season. *

Number of Crimes committed.

Year.	February to April.	May to July.	August to October.	November to January.	Total.
1860	252	283	268	146	949
1861	160	338	258	124	880
1862	194	352	236	173	955
1863	174	337	290	156	957
1864	211	394	287	172	1,064
1865	201	439	341	196	1,177
1866	227	427	311	191	1,156
1867	201	315	234	172	922
1868	187	308	224	132	851
1869	211	311	237	177	936
Ten Years.	2,018	3,504	2,686	1,639	9,847

* From Dr. Tardieu's "Étude Médico-légale sur les Attentats sur Mœurs." On this subject see also articles by *Villerme,* in "Annales d'Hygiène, 1851," and *Bernard* in "Archives de l'Anthrop. Criminelle" for 1886 and 1887.

DEMOGRAPHY

AN ARNO PRESS COLLECTION